GHOSTLY
CUMBRIA

ROB KIRKUP

The History Press

For Mam and Dad

First published 2011

The History Press
The Mill, Brimscombe Port
Stroud, Gloucestershire, GL5 2QG
www.thehistorypress.co.uk

British Library Cataloguing in Publication Data.
A catalogue record for this book is available from the British Library.

ISBN 978 0 7509 5312 5

Typesetting and origination by The History Press
Printed in Great Britain
Manufacturing managed by Jellyfish Print Solutions Ltd

Contents

Foreword   v

Acknowledgements   ix

Introduction   x

Haunted Locations in Cumbria   1

About the Author   82

Sources & Recommended Reading   83

Foreword

*G*hosts. Phantoms. Spectres. Whatever we choose to label them, nobody rightly knows what they are or indeed where they come from. Are they really the faded forms of previously living souls, perpetually walking paths that they once did when upon this mortal coil, or are they something completely different altogether? No matter what, one thing is abundantly clear; Britain has an absolute plethora of them!

From phantom battles complete with spectral soldiers, to ghostly hitchhikers who vanish into thin air from the backseat of your car, Britain has them all. It is my honest opinion that this country is the most haunted and most paranormally active on the face of the planet. Why do I say this? Because during my twenty-four years or so as a paranormal investigator and author, and via my work within the media on the subject, no other country continually amazes and fascinates me with its tales of things 'going bump in the night'. I have travelled extensively throughout this land, which sometimes appears to be a dark and foreboding one, all in the name of uncovering a ghost or two, or learning a new story. I have spent countless nights in cold and draughty castles, manor houses, pubs, inns, forts and more. I have driven thousands upon thousands of miles along the length and breadth of our roadways, some of which are haunted too! And all of this stems from the time when I was a young boy of about eleven years old.

Throughout my childhood, and on into the present day, I have read many books that have captured my imagination with the stories they contain; I am always on the lookout for something new on the horizon. I was intrigued, and curious, when the author of this very book contacted me and permitted me to read it. I did not rightly know what to expect; would this publication live up to my high expectations that were set many years before by the books I had read? I am pleased to say there was no reason to worry. In keeping with so many other good books about ghosts and the paranormal, Rob Kirkup has also managed to capture my imagination with the stories contained within, and I am sure he will do the same for those readers who will follow in my footsteps. Surprisingly, Rob has also included accounts of which I had not previously heard and that is testament in itself to the research that has gone into this publication.

Whether you are a veteran paranormal investigator or indeed someone new to the subject of ghosts and hauntings, I have no doubt that you will find this book a very interesting read.

The beautiful, yet haunting, Castlerigg Stone Circle; one of the oldest stone circles in Europe.
(By kind permission of English Heritage)

And of course, one of the best things about reading books like this one: you don't have to personally spend endless hours researching the stories, staying up late into the night, sifting through page after page of notes, or shivering endlessly on those winter days when gathering a story means braving the elements that all too frequently get thrown at us in this haunted country; Rob Kirkup has already done this for us!

So grab a warm drink, sit back in your favourite armchair and lose yourself in *Ghostly Cumbria* … if you dare!

Phil Whyman, 2011
Author and Paranormal Investigator

Acknowledgements

I'd like to begin by expressing my gratitude to my family for their support and encouragement during the writing of my fourth book; *Ghostly Cumbria*. I would particularly like to thank my wife Jo, my parents Tom and Emily, and my brother Thomas. I would also like to thank my in-laws Michael and Patricia, my brother-in-law, James, and Norman, Jo's grandfather.

Many thanks go to my good friends John Crozier and Andrew Markwell for joining me on many, many road trips, spanning literally thousands of miles to visit the locations you will read about throughout this book, and helping me to conduct research and take the photographs that you see on these very pages. All images featured in this book I photographed myself, unless otherwise stated.

I would also like to extend my thanks to the heroic farmer who saved the day when John and I went to Muncaster Castle for a Halloween ghost walk, and he towed my car out of a hole with his tractor.

My close friends have offered no end of encouragement during this project and I would like to thank them all. Especially David Henderson, Richard Stokoe, John Gray, Dan Armstrong, Paul Morton, Andrew Davidson, Brian Carmichael, Ryan Elwell, Brian Moore, Peter Slater, and Paul Bicker.

I was thrilled when Phil Whyman agreed to write the foreword for my book. His book, *Phil Whyman's Dead Haunted: Paranormal Encounters & Investigations*, published in 2007, was a brilliant guide on how to conduct a paranormal investigation, and definitely made a lasting impression on me. Thanks Phil.

I am indebted to the staff and owners of the locations included in this book; they could not have possibly been more helpful and I am grateful to them all for allowing their properties to be featured.

A number of people were kind enough to talk to me about their personal experiences at the locations that I chose to include in this book. I would like to extend my gratitude to them all; David Scanlan, Ann Winsper, Angela Chatterton, Sue Dent, Jonathan Downes, Christopher Terry and Steve Taylor.

Last, but certainly by no means least, I would like to thank everyone at the History Press, Matilda Richards, Anna O'Loughlin, and Kerry Green in particular, for the faith they have showed in me throughout the *Ghostly* series, and their support and guidance in the writing of *Ghostly Cumbria*.

Introduction

The picturesque county of Cumbria has always been viewed as a mysterious corner of England. Over 15 million visitors flock to Cumbria each year, with the natural beauty of Lake District, in particular, drawing holidaymakers from all over the world. But beneath the peaceful and serene surface is a plethora of strange, supernatural secrets. The pre-historic monuments and ancient buildings situated in Cumbria also provide the ideal haunting space for the hundreds, if not thousands, of ghosts that reside in this truly haunted county.

Cumbria has many connections with Arthurian Legend and could stake a strong claim for being the territory of King Arthur and his legendary knights. There is, in fact, a henge monument near Penrith, known as Arthur's Round Table.

The atmospheric ruins of Pendragon Castle are found in Kirkby Stephen, and are reputed to have been built by Uther Pendragon, the father of King Arthur. According to legend, Uther Pendragon and a hundred of his men were killed here when Saxon invaders poisoned the well.

According to Sir Walter Scott's poem, 'The Bridal of Triermain', written in 1813, Castle Rock of Triermain played host to King Arthur, and his daughter Gyneth was cursed to an eternal slumber by Merlin. The curse lasted for 500 years, after which she was eventually awakened by Sir Roland de Vaux. An alternative legend, also based upon Scott's poem, tells of King Arthur entertaining a group of fairies at Castle Rock and Merlin cursing one of the fairies to sleep forever more. Legends of fairies are commonplace in Cumbria and feature throughout the history of the ancient county.

The Beetham Fairy Steps are found near to Beetham Church and are cut into the limestone rock. It is said that if you can climb them without touching either side then you will be granted a wish by the fairies. Another location with links to fairy lore is Castle Howe, the site of a fairy home on the banks of Bassenthwaite Lake, near Kendal. Also a stone circle known as Elva Hill is said to be a place of fairy ritual; sadly only fifteen of the original thirty stones remain.

There are centuries of legend and folklore associated with Cumbria, and unusual occurrences continue to this very day. There are reliable reports on a weekly, possible even daily basis of encounters with ghosts and phantom creatures. One such bizarre occurrence was a little over a decade ago in 1998; Nursery Woods in Beckermet hit headlines across the country when a 7ft-tall bigfoot-type 'monster', covered from head to toe in ginger hair, was seen drinking from a pond. Apparently it then stood upright and ran off into the trees. This was followed later that year by reports of a huge winged creature flying over Nursery Woods; one of the eye witnesses described the beast as resembling a pterodactyl from illustrations they had seen in books of dinosaurs and the Jurassic Park movies.

A truly remarkable story appeared in the Cumbrian local press as I was putting the finishing touches to *Ghostly Cumbria*. On the 1 September 2010, the CCTV in the lounge of the General Wolfe Pub in Penrith captured what can only be described as a bona fide recording of a ghost. A ghostly glowing image appeared in the deserted bar at 12.18 a.m., then hovered in the air for thirty-one seconds before moving quickly and purposefully through a wall.

The landlord of the General Wolfe revealed to journalists that he has seen dark figures in the bar, and his dog has refused to go into the bar area on several occasions. The building, and the adjoining Thomas Cook travel agents, was at one time a funeral parlour. This could explain why Thomas Cook's security cameras recorded something every bit as astounding exactly one week later. The recording shows a computer mouse move across a desk in the empty office. The movement of the mouse causes a computer monitor to come on, which bathes the office in a soft light, seconds before a large sign hanging on the inside of the shop's window falls down.

Amy Dryden works in the Thomas Cook shop and, when interviewed by a local newspaper, said:

> I have found it difficult to sleep since seeing the footage. It's scary. This place used to be a funeral parlour and when I go upstairs to where we keep our brochures I often get the feeling that I'm being watched. I was amazed when I saw the CCTV from the pub next door.

All of the twenty locations you will read about within the pages of *Ghostly Cumbria* are open to the public, and each chapter contains all of the information you need to go and visit for yourself: the history, the ghost stories, opening times, contact details, and even directions to help you get there. So why not use this book to help you plot out your very own ghost trail across one of Britain's most haunted counties … if you're not too afraid?

Rob Kirkup, 2011

Haunted Locations in Cumbria

Aira Force

The most famous of the Lake District waterfalls, Aira Force, drops an impressive 66ft from beneath the arched stone footbridge, which was once a packhorse bridge. It offers a spectacular view from the top; you can see the water making its magnificent leap, sending spray high into the air. The word 'force' is used in many parts of northern England and comes from the Old Norse word *fors*.

In the 1780s, the Howard family, of nearby Greystoke Castle, owned a hunting lodge near Aira Force and renovated the lodge into what is now Lyulph's Tower. They landscaped the area around the Force, planting over half a million trees. In 1846 an arboretum was created in the area below the waterfall, with over 200 specimens of firs, pines, spruces and cedars being planted.

The poet William Wordsworth paid many visits to the area around Aira Force; it is believed he was inspired to write his poem 'Daffodils' (with the famous opening line, 'I wandered lonely as a cloud') as he saw daffodils growing along the Ullswater shore. The fall is mentioned in three of William Wordsworth's poems. In 'The Somnambulist', written in 1828, Wordsworth tells of a tragic medieval legend. The former hunting lodge at Aira Force was once the home to a girl named Emma who was engaged to a knight, Sir Eglamore. Sir Eglamore had sailed to foreign shores to do gallant deeds worthy of his true love, but months passed and he did not return. Emma grew distracted and each night she could be found sleepwalking alongside the waterfall. One night Sir Eglamore returned and, as he neared Aira Force, he could clearly see in the moonlight a white, robed figure walking silently alongside the roaring waterfall; at once he could tell it was his beloved Emma. He rushed to her and as he touched her shoulder she awoke. She saw the face of her beloved, but was so surprised that she fell backwards into the angry torrent of Aira Force. The knight jumped in to save her, and she died in his arms. The heartbroken knight built himself a hermit's cell in a nearby cave and saw out his days there alone.

Although the sad tale of Emma, and her death at the force, appears to be nothing more than a legend, there have been reported sightings of a spectral lady dressed in white at Aira Force on several occasions over the last 200 years. On one such occasion, back in 1839, a Miss Smith decided to explore Aira Force alone and successfully climbed up alongside the waterfall for about half an hour, but then she found herself trapped within a cave. She managed to find her way out but this route took her to the brink of a chasm with nowhere to go. She began to panic; all around her were rocks and she saw no exit. She considered leaping down the chasm, although she would have had little or no chance of escaping with her life. All of a

The powerful Aira Force, the Lake District's most famous waterfall.
(By kind permission of the National Trust)

sudden, around 180m in front of her, she saw a young lady dressed all in white. The young lady beckoned to Miss Smith, who followed her and immediately found a safe exit; why she had not seen the exit herself perplexed her greatly. She now found herself on the other side of the Force with the mysterious White Lady. The apparition guided Miss Smith safely to a path which led to the base of the Force. At this point the White Lady vanished.

Visitor Information

Address:
Ullswater Property Office
Tower Buildings
Watermillock
Penrith
Cumbria
CA11 0JS

Tel: (015394) 46027
Website: www.nationaltrust.org.uk/main/w-ullswaterandairaforce-2
Email: ullswater@nationaltrust.org.uk

Opening Hours: Aira Force is accessible at any reasonable time.

How to Get There: 3 miles along the A592 from Patterdale and about 150 yards from the junction with the A5091.

Additional Information:
- Aira Force has a car park with five designated disabled parking spaces
- There are toilets at Aira Force car park, Patterdale (opposite the White Lion public house) and Glenridding tourist information centre
- There are baby changing facilities in the women's toilet at Aira Force car park
- Dogs are allowed but must be kept on a lead
- There are picnic spots at Aira Force
- There are seasonal tea rooms at Aira Force and at Side Farm, also ran by the National Trust
- There is a campsite at Side Farm, tel: (017684) 82337
- Information stewards are based at Aira Force car park through the main season to offer advice and assistance
- The paths to the Victorian Glade and Aira Green are suitable for wheelchairs, but the path to the waterfall is not, due to being steep, rocky and narrow in places. The lakeshore footpath has recently been made more accessible and is classed as 'a path for many'

Beacon Hill

High above the town of Penrith is Beacon Hill, standing 937ft above sea level. Its name comes from the beacons that were lit here in times of war, as far back as 1296, when there was the constant threat of invasion from the Scots, and at which time they would have been constructed of piles of branches. Beacons were used as a warning and a distress signal to call for aid from across the north.

Beacon Tower.

Others would have been lit at Carlisle, Kirkoswald and Orton Scar. There has been a building upon the hill for over five centuries, and a signal fire was last lit during the Napoleonic wars. In 1719 the most recent monument was built and is known as Beacon Tower. It was built from sandstone taken from the hill, to replace the previous structures.

Since the late eighteenth century, Beacon Hill has also commonly been known locally as Gibbet Hill; this is as a result of one of the lowest points in the history of the district. On Tuesday, 18 November 1766, Thomas Parker, a butcher who lived in Langwathby, was returning home from Penrith market when he called in at the Cross Keys public house in Carleton. Thomas was a familiar face at the Cross Keys and he was celebrating a particularly good day's takings. He had a pleasant night, buying drinks for friends and drinking far too much himself. When he came to leave, the landlord offered Thomas a bed for the night, rather than walk home in his drunken state, but Thomas loudly declined the offer, claiming to be fine. However, Thomas never made it home; his lifeless body was found in the Langwathby road, close to the junction with the Beacon road. He had been beaten to death in a vicious attack and his purse had been taken.

In the following month a man named Thomas Nicholson, Parker's godson, was questioned about the murder and later put on trial at Carlisle Assizes. He was found guilty of Thomas Parker's murder and sentenced to be executed and hung in chains. On the 31 August 1767, a large crowd gathered to watch the condemned Thomas Nicholson as he dangled by his neck until dead. Once he was confirmed deceased, his body was cut down and placed in an iron cage that hung from a gibbet erected at the top of Beacon Hill. The Edenhall parish register includes the following documented recording of the event:

Thomas Parker, householder, November 21st. This man was found murdered on the road from Penrith to Edenhall, near the place called Nancy Dobson's Stone, on Tuesday night, the 18th of this instant, for which murder Thomas Nicholson was executed and hung in chains near the same place, August 31st 1767.

For almost seven months his body was left hanging from the gibbet as a warning to others. The clothes were soon stripped from the lifeless felon by the winter gales, and the fauna of the area began to feast on the rotting flesh. One witness to the gory scene claimed that his body appeared almost alive; such was the movement of the maggots and insect-life that were living within his corpse and eating him from the inside-out. Foxes and wild dogs would fight over the meat that dropped from the cage and within a matter of weeks the bones had been picked clean and all that was left was a skeleton, rattling eerily in the wind. On one particularly windy day in March the following year, the gibbet blew down and all that remained of Nicholson was a pile of bones. The people of Edenhall gathered the bones together and wrapped them in a winding sheet and buried them in an unmarked grave nearby.

The remote track that leads to the summit of Beacon Hill and to Beacon Tower can be very creepy, especially after dark.

Poet William Wordsworth went riding on the hill in 1775, aged only five, with a family servant called James, and they became separated. William climbed down from his small horse and stumbled upon the spot on which the gibbet had stood. A local, who had not wanted the murder of Thomas Parker to be forgotten, had cut the initials T.P.M. into the turf (Thomas Parker Murdered), and young William saw these initials. It left a lasting impression on him and he later wrote of this experience in his epic poem *The Prelude*:

> Dismounting, down the rough and stony moor
> I led my horse, and stumbling on, at length
> Came to a bottom, where in former times
> A murderer had been hung in iron chains.
> The gibbet-mast had mouldered down, the bones
> And iron case were gone; but on the turf,
> Hard by, soon after that fell deed was wrought,
> Some unknown hand had carved the murderer's name.

During harsh winter nights the ghost of Nicholson returns to Beacon Hill, his skeletal remains staring through empty eye sockets within the iron cage hanging from the gibbet arm. Other visitors to the summit of the hill have claimed to smell the overpowering stench of rotting meat; the unmistakable smell of death. Another, possibly unrelated, occurrence has been the sound of a male voice, or voices, talking quietly within Beacon Tower.

An unsubstantiated legend of the area states that in centuries past, unmarried mothers, often pregnant by their employer and fearing for their livelihood, would leave their newborn babies on Beacon Hill to die.

Visitor Information

How to Get There: From Beacon Edge the footpath to Beacon Hill is signposted.

Additional Information:

- The woodland is home to a range wildlife; keep a look out for badgers, foxes, and common lizards
- The path to the Beacon Pike is quite steep and very rocky in places, so is unsuitable for wheelchairs or pushchairs
- Substantial walking shoes are recommended
- There are no facilities at the summit of Beacon Hill

Birdoswald Roman Fort

Birdoswald is the site of the Roman fort Banna. It is the best preserved of the forts along Hadrian's Wall. Hadrian's Wall was built between AD 122 and AD 138 and was an 80-Roman-mile-long (73 modern miles) barrier between the Roman province of Britannia and the Barbarian North. It stretches from Segedunum at Wallsend, on the River Tyne in the east, to Bowness-on-Solway in the west. Hadrian's Wall was made a UNESCO (United Nations Educational, Scientific and Cultural Organization) World Heritage Site in 1987.

Along the wall were seventeen Roman forts that protected this far-flung corner of the Roman Empire. Banna is the eleventh fort from the east end of the wall and was built on a steep-sided promontory, contained to the south by a meander of the River Irthing, which took three units of soldiers six years to build. The name Banna is Latin for 'spur' or 'tongue', which reflects the location of the site. It was occupied daily by 1,000 Roman soldiers for almost 300 years, until the Roman occupation in Britain came to an end.

The extensive remains of the foundations of Birdoswald.
(By kind permission of English Heritage)

The East Gate of the fort at Birdoswald. (By kind permission of English Heritage)

The fort will have originally comprised of barrack blocks, a hospital, granaries, a basilica, a headquarters building, and the commander's house. The rectangular wall of the fort is still visible today, as are remains of the granaries and basilica.

Occupation on the site continued long after the Roman Empire fell in the late fifth century, with the existing buildings being used for many hundreds of years, until a medieval tower house was built on the site. This was replaced in the sixteenth century with a fortified bastle house, designed to protect its occupants from the Border Reivers (raiders who lived along the Anglo-Scottish border).

A farmhouse was later built around the bastle, and the site was used for farming until as recently as 1984, at which point the land passed into the hands of Cumbria County Council. In 2004, English Heritage assumed responsibility for the running of Birdoswald.

In 1821 an altar was unearthed on the site, which revealed the Roman name of the fort (Banna); the altar was dedicated to the woodland god Silvanus by the 'Venatores Bannienses', which translates as 'the hunters of Banna'. The name of Birdoswald was first used in the late twelfth century and translates as 'the farm of Oswald'.

The sounds of marching and whispering have been heard within the farmhouse.
(By kind permission of English Heritage)

The fort is said to have once been named Camboglanna, leading many to believe that this may well be the site of the fabled Camlann, where King Arthur fought his final battle in AD 537, and was fatally wounded by Mordred. These claims were strengthened between 1987 and 1992 when archaeological excavations revealed a large timber feasting hall, built in the fifth or sixth century, on the site of two Roman granaries. Tony Wilmott directed these excavations and suggested that after the Roman rule in Britain came to an end, the remains of the fort became the power base for a local warband.

In recent years Birdoswald has developed a reputation for being one of the most haunted sites in Cumbria. The modern 39-bed farmhouse, which can be booked for groups wishing to stay overnight on the site of the fort, appears to be the most active area; a variety of audible phenomena such as whispering late at night and the sounds of marching have been reported.

The section of Hadrian's Wall near Birdoswald itself was the focus of an amazing report by an American family visiting the fort in 2005. Two teenage boys spotted two people dressed in Roman garb standing next to the wall, 100m or so away from where they were stood. Assuming it to be members of staff in period costume they turned to tell their parents, but when they turned back there was no one there.

They had had a clear view; in the few seconds it had taken to turn away and turn back there was nowhere that the two figures could have gone to that would have been out of their field of vision. When they were leaving they mentioned this to the staff member on the desk of the Birdoswald visitors centre and were told that there was nobody in period dress working at the fort. It appears they had caught a glimpse of a bygone age and had actually seen the Roman soldiers who would have been stationed at the fort over 1,500 years ago.

Visitor Information

Address:
Birdoswald Roman Fort
Gilsland
Brampton
Carlisle
Cumbria
CA8 7DD

Telephone number: (016977) 47602
Website: www.english-heritage.org.uk/daysout/properties/birdoswald-roman-fort-hadrians-wall

Opening Hours:
1 April – 30 September, seven days a week including bank holidays, 10 a.m. – 5.30 p.m. (last admission 5 p.m.).

How to Get There: 4 miles west of Greenhead off the B6318. Signposted from the A69 (Carlisle-Hexham road) at Brampton roundabout.

Additional Information:
- There is a 39-bed farmhouse, which can be booked to stay in. It provides the perfect base for exploring the sites on the wall
- There is disabled parking on site. There is also disabled access to the visitor centre, toilets, shop, tearoom, and part of the site
- Car parking is chargeable, but this is refunded upon paying for entry to the fort
- There is a tearoom on site selling homemade cakes and locally-sourced produce
- Dogs are allowed providing they are kept on leads

Brougham Hall

*B*rougham Hall (pronounced 'broom') was dubbed 'the Windsor of the North' by the Victorians because of its links with royalty. King George V was a regular guest, as was King Edward VII.

The hall was originally built in the thirteenth century as a fortified manor house, founded by Gilbert de Broham. It was built upon lands rich with history; the stone hall, added in 1307 by Ricardus de Brun of Dummaloch, stands on the angle of the earlier Roman fort of Brocavum.

By the turn of sixteenth century there was a complex range of buildings, including a manor house and a gate, to which a seventeenth-century pele tower was added. In 1676 the hall was sold by the Brougham family and the estate was purchased by a Mr James Bird. However, in 1726, fifty years later, the estate was bought back into the family by John Brougham.

The hall was extended and enlarged between 1829 and 1847 by the architect Lewis Nockalls Cottingham. Further alterations were made during the 1860s.

Following the collapse of the family's fortune, Brougham Hall passed out of the family in the 1930s and began to decay and fall into ruin. During the Second World

Brougham Hall. (By kind permission of Brougham Hall)

War it became a secret weapons research centre; it was used specifically for designing a futuristic optical-light weapon for tanks, designed to temporarily blind the enemy (the blindness would last for up to two weeks). Churchill and Eisenhower both visited the ruin of Brougham Hall during this period. The substantial remains of the once prosperous Brougham Hall, are currently the subject of a restoration project which has been ongoing since January 1986.

There have been numerous reports in recent years of strange happenings at the ancient manor house and paranormal investigators and mediums have claimed that Brougham Hall may contain a doorway to the spirit world. Groups of shadowy figures have been seen, watches and clocks stop, footsteps have been heard, as has laughing. Inexplicable sounds are often heard echoing around the hall, and objects have been seen by several witnesses moving of their own accord.

I spoke with the owner of Brougham Hall, Christopher Terry, about the hall's links to the paranormal; 'Yes, Brougham Hall has a haunting history going back to Victorian times, long before the current craze of paranormal investigations started,' he commented.

A Second World War air-raid shelter. Visitors have complained of batteries in cameras and mobile phones draining within seconds here. (By kind permission of Brougham Hall)

One haunting that dates back to Victorian times is that of a tall man with piercing eyes and a wheezing chest. He has been captured on photos in more recent years and seems to enjoy being seen. He was especially fond of scaring women that worked at the hall by whispering in their ear, or stroking their arm. One scribe at the time wrote about the spirit and revealed that it was believed to be a man who was charged of raping three women before being beaten to death by an angry group of local men in Penrith. The name of the man has been lost to history.

The most famous story from the annals of Brougham Hall's long history is the legend of an unknown warrior's skull, which was bricked up inside a wall to bring luck and prosperity to the Brougham family. The 2nd Lord Brougham wrote of his discovery of a skull, sword, and spur found within a wall; it seems likely that this is the same skull as the one referred to in the legend but we can never be sure. The legend says that many years ago, the skull was removed from the hall and the family suffered the most terrifying, haunting disturbances and torment. It was quickly returned to the hall and reinterred within the wall, at which point peace was restored to Brougham Hall.

Over the centuries that followed, the legendary tale of Brougham Hall's skull was passed down from generation to generation of the Brougham family, and retold countless times, with all believing it to be nothing more than the legend it appeared to be. However, it appears that it may be far, far more than just a story, as

The Brougham door knocker. Four examples of this twelfth-century design exist; two in Durham and two in Brougham. (By kind permission of Brougham Hall)

The statue of Jesus Christ on the cross in the Lord Chancellor's Den. The statue lies flat, so Jesus will forever look to the heavens. (By kind permission of Brougham Hall)

Christopher Terry explained to me a grisly discovery made during the restoration process:

> I can certainly vouch for the existence of the skull because during the restoration process we came across it; it was very green in colour. We made sure it was reinterred within the 58in-thick wall, exactly where we had found it. The skull had been poleaxed; there was an equilateral triangle of small holes in the top of the skull. I showed the skull to my dentist and it was the skull of a male aged about thirty-five years old.

A stone epitaph, including all the details known about the skull, was carved in homage to the unknown warrior and is visible today on the wall of a small room. The inscription is copied from an earlier one of an unknown date and reads, 'Unknown soldier from a sunlit shore, who paid the price in an unknown war. For an unknown God in an unknown time, may peace eternal now be thine. Pray lie within this ancient wall, and guard that it should never fall.'

On the 19 December 1745 the English defeated the Scots at the Battle of Clifton Moor. This took place very close to the hall and, ever since, the sounds of battle have been heard in and around the hall in the dead of night; horses galloping, the clash of blade on blade, and the screams and moans of people dying.

The Lord Chancellor's Den is an overgrown area featuring a sculpture of Jesus Christ on the cross. Visitors have reported the feeling of being watched when on this site. A medium picked up on a woman crying at the foot of the statue, as her son, a young boy in his early teens, was begging his mother to help him; apparently, the medium said, he had been struck across the head with a blunt object and killed as a sacrifice in the room that was here. The medium added that the statue was not in this area at the time of the murder, and that the woman will forever remain at Brougham Hall, unable to find peace from the experience of seeing her young son killed before her eyes, helpless to prevent it.

During a paranormal investigation at the hall in January 2009, a medium sensed the spirit of a fifteen-year-old boy called James, who fell to his death while working on the hall; his body was hidden and his death covered up. The medium also picked up on a lady who had been carried to the top of a tower by soldiers and thrown to her death.

I spoke to Angela Chatterton, of the Grey Ladies Team, who investigated Brougham Hall, and particularly one of the shops now situated there, on 18 April 2009. She shared with me the terrifying results:

> We arrived at Brougham Hall on a dry, sunny afternoon, so took advantage by taking lots of outside photos which captured the history of the location before dark. The Grey Ladies team were invited to join the Mostly Ghostly team from Dumfries along with a couple of local residents.
>
> The most amazing activity occurred during our final vigil of the night. We had all felt some sort of energy was building up in the furniture shop earlier in the evening, so headed back. As we approached the furniture Shop, our EMF meter suddenly went crazy outside. It was clear that some kind of energy level had built up around this shop, so we had no option but to go inside for our final vigil. We nervously huddled

The restoration of Brougham Hall has been ongoing since 1986. (By kind permission of Brougham Hall)

round the large centre table, having set up cameras and other equipment around the shop. People started to note the room temperature was dropping, so I asked if any spirits were with us. Immediately, a loud bang was made on the shop window and the EMF (electromagnetic fields) meter started to screech, which was lying in the middle of the table. We could not get it to switch off and the noise lasted for ten minutes. This event became our best ever investigation moment, as it really did feel like we had witnessed something genuinely paranormal, without putting it down to the weather elements or someone walking about. By this time, it was approaching 2 a.m., so we called it a night, packed up and left on a high from the evening's amazing events.

Visitor Information

Address:
Brougham Hall
Penrith
Cumbria
CA10 2DE

Telephone number: (01768) 868184
Website: www.broughamhall.co.uk

Opening Hours: The opening hours are informal, but generally it is open from 9 a.m. – 6 p.m. every day. The Fusion Café is open from 9 a.m. – 4 p.m. every day (except Tuesdays, during the winter).

How to Get There: Brougham Hall is 1 mile south of Penrith, just off the A6 on the B6262. If coming from Penrith, follow the signs for the A6 to Shap. You will cross Eamont Bridge and go over a small roundabout, then you will see Brougham Hall signposted to the left.

Additional Information:
- Entry is free of charge but a donation of £4 per adult and £2 for children is asked for to assist in the restoration of Brougham Hall
- There are toilet facilities at Brougham Hall
- Brougham Hall offers a perfect location for events such as weddings, corporate events, outdoor music and theatre
- Private tours for groups and individuals are available on request
- Brougham Hall is home to an array of small businesses, arts and crafts workshops and studios, including a country furnishing shop, a finance specialist, a holistic therapy centre, a cycle touring company and much more

Carlisle Castle

Carlisle Castle was first built on a sandstone bluff between the River Eden and the River Caldew during the reign of William II of England. At that time, north and west Cumbria was known as the county town of Cumberland, and was still considered a part of Scotland. King William II, the son of William the Conqueror, drove the Scots out of Cumberland on his arrival and claimed the area for England. There was a need to keep the northern border of England secure from the threat of the invading Scots, so, in 1092, William II ordered work to begin on a castle. The castle was of an earthen and wood style, built upon the site of a series of Roman forts (dating between the first and fourth centuries) that had served the western end of Hadrian's Wall.

In 1122, Henry I visited Cumberland and ordered that the castle be refortified in stone and that a keep be constructed. However, work did not begin on the stone keep until 1132 and, in 1135, King David I of Scotland seized the castle; Cumberland was once more under Scottish rule. Under David I, the castle keep was completed and city walls were added. In 1157, Henry II of England fought the Scots and won Cumberland back. He then added curtain walls to the castle as an extra layer of protection.

The castle changed hands again in 1216 under the command of Alexander II. It suffered considerable damage in the course of this conflict and the following battles, which saw the English fighting to reclaim Cumberland. In the mid-thirteenth century the English succeeded in retaking Carlisle Castle, but it was now a ruin.

The ancient fortress of Carlisle Castle. (By kind permission of English Heritage)

The Great Hall. (By kind permission of English Heritage)

In around 1280, King Edward I, known as Edward Longshanks, ordered that Scottish prisoners at Carlisle Castle should be incarcerated with chains around their necks and placed upon a ledge. The prisoner would try in vain to fend off tiredness and sleep, but inevitably each and every one of them would succumb to exhaustion and fall asleep, resulting in them falling from the ledge and hanging themselves by the tight chain around their neck.

Repairs were carried out on the castle at the end of the thirteenth century and, in 1306 – 1307, the castle was used as the seat of government for the English Parliament. Further repairs were carried out between 1378 and 1383

Between the 18 May and 13 July 1568, two months after her abdication of the Scottish Throne, Mary Queen of Scots was imprisoned within the castle. She was held in a tower in the south-east corner, which became known as Mary's Tower, but has since been demolished.

In 1644, during the English Civil War, the castle was besieged by the Parliamentary forces for eight months. The garrison finally surrendered to the Scots after running out of food, forcing them to resort to eating their dogs, rats and eventually their horses. The castle was retaken by the King in 1648.

The final battle ever on English soil, and the most important one for the city of Carlisle and its castle, was during the second Jacobite uprising against George II, in 1745. The forces of Prince Charles Edward Stuart, affectionately known as Bonnie Prince Charlie, travelled south from Scotland into England, reaching as far south as Derby. Carlisle and the castle were seized and fortified by the Jacobites. However, they were driven north by the forces of William Augustus, Duke of Cumberland. Carlisle was recaptured, and 127 Jacobites were jailed and held in a room on the first floor of the Keep. The desperate prisoners were led by their survival instincts and licked the stones in the wall in order to get moisture, but two men perished within that cell before a sentence could be passed. The remaining prisoners were found guilty and sentenced to death. The condemned were placed on black hurdles and dragged through the streets where the decapitated heads of their fallen comrades were displayed. The men were hung on Gallows Hill, but cut down just before they took their last breath. They were then sliced open and had their entrails ripped out and burnt before their very eyes and then, finally, they had their heads cut off.

Some parts of the castle were then demolished for use as raw materials in the nineteenth century, leaving the castle as it stands today. The army moved in to take hold of the castle, which was the regimental depot of the Border Regiment until control passed to the Department of Environment in 1959, and then later to English Heritage, who still manage the castle today.

The impressive fortress has bore witness to a great deal of death, torture, and suffering in the last 900 years; it comes as little surprise that all too regularly the ghosts of soldiers are seen and the screams of the once incarcerated reverberate within the stone walls of Carlisle Castle.

One of the spectral soldiers reported at Carlisle Castle may well be that of a sergeant, who committed suicide by hanging himself from a beam in the castle in the 1800s. In the years that followed, his former colleagues would often report seeing him walking silently throughout the Keep.

In 1820, the skeletal remains of a lady was found bricked up within one of the walls of the Captain's Tower. Three valuable rings remained on her fingers and she was still partially clothed in scraps of a tartan dress. It is unknown who she is, but evidence indicated that when she was walled up she was still alive. The grisly discovery seems to have disturbed her spirit and she now haunts the castle, forever searching for whoever bricked her up to die within that wall. She is blamed for an incident that occurred three years later in 1823; a soldier was patrolling when he was suddenly confronted by the mysterious figure of a woman. She did not move or speak when he challenged her, so he lunged at her with his bayonet. The blade met no resistance; to his abject horror it simply passed straight through her and struck the stone of the wall.

The figure then vanished before his eyes. He was found shortly afterwards in a state of shock and he revealed his account to fellow soldiers. A few hours later he died.

In 1992, the alarms went off in the King's Own Border Regiment Museum three nights in a row, indicating something had moved underneath the arch between the downstairs exhibition and the gift shop area. The building that the museum occupies is said to have once been a chapel, and the area of movement is believed to have been a crypt at one time.

In the first floor of the Keep is the room in which the Jacobites were imprisoned in 1745, evident by the 'licking stones' that remain to this day. There is said to be a malevolent spirit active within the room; it appears to have a dislike for everyone and, according to reports, staff and visitors have been mysteriously pushed and scratched.

The Captain's Tower is haunted by the spirit of an unknown woman who was bricked up alive within one of the walls. (By kind permission of English Heritage)

The Keep. (By kind permission of English Heritage)

Visitor Information

Address:
Carlisle Castle
Carlisle
Cumbria
CA3 8UR

Telephone number: (0870) 3331181
Email: customers@english-heritage.org.uk
Website: www.english-heritage.org.uk/daysout/properties/carlisle-castle

Opening Hours:
01 Apr to 30 Sep:	9.30 a.m. – 5 p.m.
01 Oct to 23 Dec:	10 a.m. – 4 p.m.
27 Dec to 31 Dec:	10 a.m. – 4 p.m.
02 Jan to 31 Mar:	10 a.m. – 4 p.m.

These dates may change annually, so please consult the website or contact English Heritage for precise dates.

How to Get There: The castle is located in the centre of Carlisle and is signposted throughout the city centre.

Additional Information:
- Dogs on leads only in restricted areas
- The castle is suitable for wheelchair access, but the interior is not accessible
- There is only parking for disabled visitors, but there is plenty of city-centre parking nearby
- Groups should pre-book
- Guided tours are available for a small charge. There are a number of tours including the Ghosts and Ghastly Stories Tour. All tours are listed on the website and advance booking is required
- There is a picnic area and a gift shop

Cartmel Priory Gatehouse

William Marshall, Lord of Cartmel and later Earl of Pembroke, founded Cartmel Priory in 1189 for a community of Augustinian canons. Building was completed in 1233 and in around 1340 an outer wall was built for the priory and a gatehouse was also added. The gatehouse was built to fortify the main entrance following raids on the area by the Scots, led by King Robert the Bruce, in 1315 and 1322.

In 1536, the priory was closed by King Henry VIII during the Dissolution of the Monasteries. Large sections of the priory buildings were sold and others were destroyed. Only the south aisle of the priory, which would become the parish church, and the gatehouse survived. It is believed that the gatehouse was spared because the Great Room within it was used as the manor court for the priors dealing with disputes over land in the area owned by the priory. It was during this period that the gatehouse was also used as a prison.

The gatehouse had many uses in the centuries that followed. Between 1624 and 1790 it functioned as the local grammar school and an adjoining cottage was built for the schoolmaster. Names of some of the children that attended school here can still be seen in the Great Room, etched into the stone wall.

During the nineteenth century the gatehouse and adjoining cottage were used to house village shops. In the early twentieth century the gatehouse was opened as a small local museum, used for exhibitions and meetings. In 1946 the Pearson family, who had earlier restored the gatehouse, gave the building to the National Trust to ensure that it would be preserved for future generations. They also sold the cottage to the National Trust for £300.

In the 1980s the Great Room was used as an art gallery. Today the gatehouse and adjoining cottage are let out to tenants as accommodation, but the National Trust are keen to ensure that the public are still able to visit this historic building, so there is an agreement in place that the Great Room will be open to the public for six afternoons each year.

A rumour that a man in a tall hat can be seen moving mysteriously in the area of the gatehouse has attracted paranormal enthusiasts. His identity is unknown, but he disappears if spoken to.

Before the railways were invented, crossing the sands of Morecambe Bay was a perilous journey, so the monks from Cartmel Priory acted as guides to passing horse-drawn carriages. Many people didn't have the money for a horse and carriage, or the assistance of a guide, so would gamble with their lives and attempt to walk across, hopeful of dodging the tide and the quicksands, both of which would kill someone on foot in minutes, and would engulf a horse and carriage within twenty minutes. Many people drowned and their bodies would be discovered by the monks, who would drag them to Cartmel Priory where they would be buried. Countless

The priory gatehouse.
(Photograph provided by Matthew Emmott – www.matthewpemmott.co.uk)

others were buried alive, sucked beneath the sand and never discovered. Figures have been seen across the sands ever since and are believed to be the spirits of those who lost their lives here. Other figures are described as being hooded; perhaps these are spirits of the monks who dedicated their lives to ensuring the safety of others.

There is also a tragic legend associated with nearby Cartmel Fell. On two farms in Cartmel lived families who were to be connected by marriage. The husband-to-be was a charcoal burner and one fateful day, as he sat on a rock outside of his hut, he was stuck by lightning and died instantly. After his funeral Kitty, his heartbroken fiancé, went to his hut and would never leave it alive again. She sat day and night calling out her lover's name. Her family tried to persuade her to come home but she refused, so they cared for her by bringing her food and blankets. Almost a year after Kitty's lover had died some men came with food for her, but when they called her name and she did not respond they entered the hut and found her dead.

The hut has long since been destroyed, but people on Cartmel Fell have seen the ghostly figure of a young woman sat upon a stone and others have heard a woman's voice carried on the breeze.

Visitor Information

Address:
Cartmel Priory Gatehouse
The Square
Cartmel
Grange-over-Sands
Cumbria
LA11 6QB

Telephone number: (01524) 701178
Email: cartpriorygatehouse@nationaltrust.org.uk
Website: www.nationaltrust.org.uk/main/w-cartmelpriorygatehouse

Opening Hours: The Great Room is open for six afternoons each year. For opening dates and times use the details above.

How to Get There: The priory gatehouse is in the centre of Cartmel, which is signposted from Grange-over-Sands.

Additional Information:
- Admission is free, but donations are welcomed
- Wheelchair access to the Great Room is not possible

Castlerigg Stone Circle

*E*very year thousands of visitors come to paint and photograph the breathtaking monument of Castlerigg Stone Circle. Others come simply to marvel at this astonishing feat of prehistoric man, dating back to around 3200 BC (the beginning of the later Neolithic period), and wonder why, how, and by whom it was built.

Although we may never truly understand the origins of Castlerigg Stone Circle, it is widely accepted that it was used for ceremonial or religious purposes, as precise alignments with the sun, moon and stars have been discovered. However, this is not conclusive evidence of why, over 5,000 years ago, many hundreds of people would spend years moving 10 ton (or more) boulders, using only ropes made of twisted bark, to this particular spot.

The circle measures around a third of an acre. Originally there were forty-two stones; now thirty-eight remain, all of various sizes and shapes. The tallest stone is 2.3m high and the heaviest stone is estimated to weigh in excess of 16 tons. Just inside the eastern side of the circle is a rectangle of ten stones known as a cove, the purpose of which is unknown.

Castlerigg Stone Circle was bought in 1913 by Canon Hardwicke Rawnsley, co-founder of the National Trust. Many visitors have noticed that Castlerigg Stone Circle has an unusual atmosphere, no doubt aided by the dramatic backdrop of the towering Cumbrian fells that surround the ancient stone circle. There are regular reports of strange blue lights that appear to dart from stone to stone (it is worth noting that this is a fairly common sighting at stone circles across the UK). It is unknown if this is a natural occurrence caused by the rocks, or if it is something otherworldly; perhaps the unusual lights are the result of some ancient ritual.

An eye-witness account by a Mr T. Singleton, published in 1919 in *English Mechanic* magazine, describes his encounter with strange white lights when walking at Castlerigg Stone Circle late at night:

> When we were at a point near which the track branches off to the Druidical circle, we all at once saw a rapidly moving light as bright as the acetylene lamp of a bicycle, and we instinctively stepped to the road-boundary wall to make way for it, but nothing came. As a matter of fact the light travelled at right angles to the road, say 20ft above our level, possibly 200 yards or so away. It was a white light and, having crossed the road, it suddenly disappeared. Whether it went out or passed behind an obstruction it is impossible to say, as I have not yet had an opportunity of again visiting the place during daylight. There is certainly no crossroads there. We then saw a number of lights, possibly a third of a mile away, directly in the direction of the Druidical circle, but of course much fainter, no doubt due to distance, moving backwards and forwards horizontally; we stood watching them for a long time, and then only left as it was so late at the hotel people might think we were lost on the mountains.

Whilst we were watching a remarkable incident happened: one of the lights, and only one, came straight to the spot where we were standing; at first very faint, as it approached the light increased in intensity. When it came quite near I was in no doubt whether I should stoop below the boundary wall as the light would pass directly over our heads. But when it came close to the wall it slowed down, stopped, quivered, and slowly went out, as if the matter producing the light had become exhausted. It was globular, white, with a nucleus possibly 6ft or so in diameter, and just high enough above the ground to pass over our heads.

There have been reports in recent years by visitors, both during daylight and after darkness has fallen, of chanting coming from within the stone circle.

Superstition holds that if you attempt to count the stones you will get a different number each time. The National Trust information board at the monument has the official number of stones listed as 40. There is also a local tradition of making a wish while standing in the centre of the circle.

Visitor Information

Address:
Castlerigg Stone Circle
Castlerigg
Keswick
Cumbria
CA12 4TE

Website: www.english-heritage.org.uk/daysout/properties/castlerigg-stone-circle

Opening Hours: Castlerigg Stone Circle is accessible at any reasonable time.
How to Get There: 1.5 miles east of Keswick, off the A66 Penrith road. The stone circle is well signposted from all directions.

Additional Information:
- Dogs are allowed on leads
- There is parking at Castlerigg Stone Circle, but during the summer months it's not uncommon for these spaces to fill up quickly. Alternative parking can be found in Keswick town centre
- There are no facilities at the site
- There are three separate self-closing accessible gates for wheelchair-users
- The circle is approximately 100m across a grass field, up a slight incline. Wheelchair users may require assistance

Dalston Hall Hotel

*T*he land on which Dalston Hall Hotel stands is steeped in over 1,500 years of history, evidenced by the Roman remains that are still visible in the area. The land was granted to the Dalston family in 1301 by Robert de Meschines, Earl of Cumberland. The Dalstons spent the 200 years that followed helping to defend the borderlands in regular raids by the Scots, often joining the garrison at Carlisle Castle. By 1500 the family's fortunes had increased and it was at this time that work began on Dalston Hall. It began life as a pele tower, built by the first John Dalston, who dedicated it to his beloved wife, Elizabeth, who he married in 1507. Elizabeth was from a wealthy family and her father owned the Manors of Kirkbride and Dockerey.

After the Dissolution of the Monasteries, John's son, Thomas, increased the family's land by buying six manors and various monastic lands. As the family's wealth increased the hall was extended with buildings added to the east and the west. During the Civil War, Dalston Hall, with its fortified pele tower, became the headquarters of Parliamentarian General David Leslie, a siege which saw much bloodshed at the hall and in the surrounding area.

The final member of the Dalston family to live in the hall was Sir George Dalston. Having no male heir, he sold the estate in 1761 for £5,060 to a grocer based in London. Sir George died four years later in 1765.

In 1897 the estate was sold to Edmund Wright Stead, who carried out extensive restoration work on the interior of Dalston Hall and constructed the entrance side of the building. A leading antiquarian of the day wrote that the result was 'a magnificent mansion surpassing perhaps even its ancient glories.'

Dalston Hall Hotel at dusk. (Photograph provided courtesy of Dalston Hall Hotel)

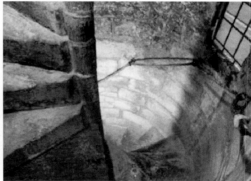

The ghost of a woman has been seen floating up this spiral staircase. (Photograph provided courtesy of Dalston Hall Hotel)

In recent years the hall was used as a private house for a time and then became a youth training centre. In 1971 it was converted into a hotel.

Dalston Hall Hotel is a luxurious retreat, set in beautiful grounds on the northern edge of the Lake District National Park. However, after dark the floodlit hotel seems to come alive with the ghosts of people long gone, some of which died peaceful deaths and felt an attachment to the building throughout their life, and others who died in the most violent of circumstances. The hotel has found notoriety in recent years as one of the most paranormally active buildings in Cumbria, if not the entire country, with reported sightings of full spectral apparitions on almost a daily basis.

After passing through the reception of the hotel you enter the Baronial Hall, dating from around 1500. This is one of the most ancient areas of the hotel, as well as the most haunted. There is an inscription on the wall which reads, 'John Dalston Elisabet mi wyf mad ys bylding'; it is in gothic script and is written in reverse. Music, laughter and excited talking has been heard coming from the empty hall in the dead of night. Candles have been seen to light themselves by astonished members of staff.

Overlooking the Baronial Hall is the Minstrel's Gallery. A woman in Tudor dress has been seen here; she is seen so regularly in fact that hotel staff have named her Lady Jane. She was a teenage maidservant who fell in love with a married gardener at the hall and was found dead after a passionate affair. It is unknown whether she was murdered or if she committed suicide, although mediums to the hall have suggested that she threw herself from the pele tower when the gardener called an end to their affair. Sightings of a woman on the balcony have also been reported, but she is unusual in that only the bottom half of her is seen. It is unknown if this is Lady Jane or another spirit altogether.

Near the bottom of the staircase is a heavy iron gate which dates back to the original fifteenth-century part of the hall, and the figure of a man has been seen standing on the other side of the gate. He never moves, he just stands totally still before fading away.

The spiral staircase ascends to the top of the tower and the figure of a woman has been seen floating up the stairs. Disembodied footsteps on the stone steps have been heard on countless occasions.

The hotel's library was once a chapel and the room is plagued with the sound of cries and dogs barking, seeming to come from the cellars which run below the room. The sounds of barrels being rolled around in the cellars have also been reported in the middle of the night. The extensive cellars wind beneath the building like a rabbit warren, and date from each period of the building's history, indicated from the different stone used throughout. It is in the cellars that that a truly terrifying spirit resides, an entity known as 'Mr Fingernails'. Several mediums who have visited the hall have independently made contact with Mr Fingernails, a nickname first given to him by a group of paranormal investigators who had an encounter with him in 2004. He is described as being a non-human entity that exudes a sense of pure evil. He appears in the form of a dark fog and can rise up from the cellar through the floor. He has long bony fingers with long, sharp, claw-like nails which earned him his nickname. One medium that made contact with the creature was physically attacked, leaving painful scratches. He removed his shirt to reveal three deep marks the length of his chest.

Another spirit believed to haunt the cellars is nicknamed 'the handyman'. This nickname comes from an occurrence during the 1960s when a workman was servicing the boilers in the cellar. A friendly man, with a large physical frame and tweed trousers, had come over and said hello. He kindly passed the tools to the workman until his work was finished. Before leaving, the workman visited the reception to thank them for sending someone down to help him. However, staff were unaware of anyone else in the hall at the time and nobody could account for the mysterious man.

Room 4 is home to one of the most commonly reported sightings at Dalston Hall Hotel; the lonely figure of a young lady standing at the window in this room, staring out into the night. She is known as 'Sad Emily' and is attired in a white dress, drawn tightly at the waist, and a white headband. She has a ring on her finger, which she plays with as she stares out into the darkness outside. An older lady comes into the room, speaks to her as if comforting her, and then she leaves. Mediums who have picked up on this spirit have claimed she is waiting for her true love, a man who never returned to her, so she will wait for him for all eternity. Lady Jane has been seen in Room 4, sitting by the fireplace, and has also been blamed for some guests waking during the night to find that their bedding has been taken off them and folded neatly at the bottom of the bed while they were asleep.

Guests in Room 4 have often reported waking up with a feeling of abject terror, convinced someone, or something, is watching them. Some guests have been so scared they have gone to reception during the night asking to be moved to another room.

In Room 12 the sound of giggling girls has been heard coming from the bathroom. The room has the best view of the gardens of any room in the hotel, and several witnesses have reported an elegant female figure walking through the gardens at night.

The corridor outside rooms 4, 5 and 6 was the scene of a murder. A young woman was taken from a party taking place in the Baronial Hall, and dragged by her hair by a large man; she was beaten up, raped and then thrown from a window to her death. There are regular reports of a 'dragging sound' in the early hours of the morning by the residents to rooms 4, 5 and 6.

In Room 6 visitors have reported the terrifying sight of the wardrobe door opening and a female form walking out of the inky blackness into the room. To the guest's utter horror she then climbs into bed with them. When the panicked guest reaches for the light switch she vanishes at the moment the light comes on.

In Room 9 violent banging on the wall has been heard; it is so forceful that it makes the mirror move. Some guests have said it seems like banging on all four of the walls simultaneously. Light bulbs frequently blow in this room as well.

In Room 19 guests have woken to see the dark figure of a man standing over them. Mediums who have come to the hall have suggested that this spirit is benevolent, but considers the room to be his own and doesn't like guests invading his space. Footsteps have been heard walking past the room, and apparently it sounds like they are walking on a stone floor, despite the floor outside the room being carpeted.

In all of the bedrooms there have been reports of electrical items such as televisions, kettles and lights turning themselves on and off during the night. It does appear that paranormal activity at Dalston Hall Hotel is widespread, with ghostly characters and strange forces at work at every turn.

Visitor Information

Address:
Dalston Hall
Dalston
Carlisle
Cumbria
CA5 7JX

Telephone number: (01228) 710271
Email: enquiries@dalstonhall.com
Website: www.dalston-hall-hotel.co.uk

How to Get There: Leave the M6 at Junction 42 (signposted for Dalston), then follow signposts for Dalston village; Dalston Hall is signposted on the right.

Additional Information:
- If you feel brave enough to spend the night at Dalston Hall Hotel, you have a choice of thirteen individually designed suites and bedrooms
- Dalston Hall Hotel is available for business gatherings and conferences with a wide selection of meeting rooms and facilities
- Diners are treated to a wide selection of English and Continental haute cuisine, complemented by a wide selection of fine wines. Alternatively the Grill Room offers a more informal setting
- Dalston Hall Hotel is licensed for civil wedding ceremonies, which can take place in the Baronial Hall or outdoors in a beautiful sandstone gazebo

Furness Abbey

*F*urness Abbey is situated in the lush wooded vale of the Valley of the Deadly Nightshade, between Dalton-in-Furness and Barrow-in-Furness.

In 1124, Stephen, Count of Boulogne and later King of England, founded an abbey near Preston in Lancashire for the order of Savigny (an order of monks that was established in Normandy). Three years later they moved north to Furness and Furness Abbey was built using only local sandstone.

Furness Abbey. (By kind permission of English Heritage)

In 1147, despite the resistance of the then Abbot, Peter of York, the abbey became a Cistercian monastery. In the decades that followed the Cistercians enlarged and rebuilt the original church. It was given a generous endowment and over the years the wealth and power grew; they owned 55,000 acres of land including most of southern Cumbria, as well as land in Ireland and the Isle of Mann. One of the kings of Mann, Reginald I, was buried at Furness Abbey. By the sixteenth century it was one of the richest Cistercian monasteries in England, second only to Fountains Abbey.

The abbey suffered many raids by the Scots, and the early twelfth century was a particularly turbulent time. It was attacked in 1316 and again in 1322, when the Low Furness area was the target of raiding parties from Scotland. The abbey itself managed to buy itself protection, but the surrounding countryside and settlements were still sacked and pillaged. As a response to this raid, Piel Castle was built nearby.

On the 9 April 1537, Furness Abbey was disestablished at the command of Henry VIII during the Dissolution of the Monasteries. Furness was one of the first of the large abbeys to be dissolved, partially due to some of the monks at Furness becoming involved in Pilgrimage of Grace, a rebellion which began in York in 1536, and partly down to the fact that Furness had openly questioned Henry VIII's declaration of supremacy over the church. The Deed of Surrender was signed in the chapter house by Roger Pele, the last abbot. Following the dissolution of Furness Abbey, it was stripped of its treasures and anything of worth, including the lead from the roof and much of its stonework, leaving the ruin that remains today.

Furness Abbey is today owned by English Heritage, and visitors can see the remains of the east end and west tower of the church, the ornately decorated chapter house and the cloister buildings.

The spirit of a monk has been seen walking towards the gatehouse before vanishing into a wall. A ghostly monk has also been seen climbing one of the staircases within the abbey; it is unknown if this is the same spirit.

There is also the ghost of a White Lady. This tragic shade is believed to be of a squire's daughter, who met her lover in secret at the ruined abbey in the years following its dissolution. One day her partner took a journey which led him out to sea and he never returned. It is said that she went back to the abbey every day until her death to take in the site she and her partner once loved; the track they used to walk along hand-in-hand is still known as 'My Lady's Walk'.

The best known, and most terrifying, of Furness Abbey's ghosts is that of a headless monk on horseback, who rides underneath the sandstone arch near the Abbey Tavern. The death of this individual is linked to the invasion by the Scots in 1316.

Visitor Information

Address:
Furness Abbey
Barrow-in-Furness
Cumbria
LA13 0PJ

Telephone number: (0870) 3331181
Email: customers@english-heritage.org.uk
Website: www.english-heritage.org.uk/daysout/properties/furness-abbey

Opening Hours:
01 Apr to 30 Jun: 10 a.m. – 5 p.m.
01 Jul to 31 Aug: 10 a.m. – 5 p.m.
01 Sep to 30 Sep: 10 a.m. – 5 p.m.
01 Oct to 23 Dec: 10 a.m. – 4 p.m.
02 Jan to 31 Mar: 10 a.m. – 5 p.m.

Opening dates may change annually; consult the website for further information.

How to Get There: The abbey is located 1.5 miles north of Barrow-in-Furness, off the A590.

Additional Information:
- Dogs allowed on leads in restricted areas only
- There is a gift shop and also refreshments and snacks are on sale
- There is a picnic ground in the abbey
- There is a pub close to the entrance
- Parking is available at the abbey
- The abbey is suitable for visitors in wheelchairs, although some assistance may be needed to access areas of the abbey ruins

Gosforth Hall Hotel

*T*he building of Gosforth Hall commenced in 1658 and was designed for Robert and Isabel Copley. The Copleys were very careful with their money; to greatly reduce building costs they took timbers from the hull of a shipwreck, from the Irish Sea, to beam the upper floors. Another example of their cost-cutting came in 1665 when Robert Copley refused to pay the herald's fee for his family coat of arms and, instead, designed his own, which is seen today in the bar of the hotel.

The building, today, is a popular hotel and remains almost entirely the same as the original structure built over 350 years ago, with the exception of a wing which was destroyed by fire. From the moment you step foot through the doorway, the low doorways and uneven floors exude the age of Gosforth Hall Hotel, as does the original solid stone spiral staircase, the steps of which are worn from centuries of use. The lounge, which was originally the kitchen, contains the widest sandstone hearth in Britain.

The staircase appears to be a focal point of Gosforth Hall Hotel's paranormal activity, as several members of staff and a number of visitors have reported hearing a baby crying on the stairs. When this occurrence is investigated, there is never anything to be found and the crying stops suddenly. There have also been reports of a foul smell on the staircase which seems to last for up to half an hour at a time. Drainage experts have been called but the location of the smell cannot be identified.

Gosforth Hall Hotel. (By kind permission of Gosforth Hall Hotel)

However, the smell does not build up; it appears in an instant and vanishes just as quickly.

The beer cellar is across a small yard from the hotel and is always locked. However, there have been instances of gas taps turning themselves off inexplicably.

The hotel itself has also got a unique paranormal oddity in the form of a haunted rocking chair. It rocks itself backwards and forwards twenty to thirty times then suddenly stops. Curious members of staff have tried to push the chair to see if the occurrence is a result of an uneven floor, but the chair only rocks three or four times before stopping.

Room 11 has a priest's hole which leads to the fireplace in the bar. In the seventeenth century, it was illegal to be a Catholic and martyrs of the faith were killed by the crown authorities for their beliefs. Robert and Isabel were devout Catholics and risked their own lives by giving shelter to Catholic priests, to help them escape persecution. Visitors to the room have seen a figure resembling a friar or monk sitting by the entrance to the priest's hole. Guests to Room 11 have also seen a strange pale face peering in through the window.

The bar is another paranormal hotspot. Staff members and guests have witnessed glasses and tankards being thrown from the bar. There have also been sightings of an old man who appears to glide through the bar room. It is believed it may be the spirit of Robert Copley, unable to leave the building that he loved so much in life.

Other reports suggest something paranormal about the timbers of the upper floors; they are said to groan with the anguish of the seamen who clung to them as they died in the icy waters.

Next to the hotel is the Church of St Mary's, which contains a wealth of early Christian relics. The church has been rebuilt several times and there is evidence of a church being here as far back as the early ninth century. The church is famed for the Gosforth Cross, a 14ft-tall, slender Viking cross dating from around 900, depicting a mixture of Norse and Christian imagery. Originally it is thought that there were four such crosses within

The Gosforth Cross within the graveyard of St Mary's Church.

the churchyard; two were destroyed completely and the third was broken up in the eighteenth century and turned into a sundial.

There are two hogback grave stones within the church, known as the Saint's Stone and the Warrior's Stone, which are said to be the original grave stones of an early saint and a Viking warrior. It is possible that the spirit of the Viking Warrior has been unable to rest in peace, as locals passing the church on clear moonlit nights have seen a dark figure moving silently between the gravestones. Some witnesses claim that the figure was clutching an object in its hand which resembled a long sword, glinting in the moonlight.

Visitor Information

Address:
Gosforth Hall Hotel
Gosforth
Cumbria
CA20 1AZ

Telephone number: (019467) 25322
Email: info@gosforthhallhotel.co.uk
Website: www.gosforthhallhotel.co.uk

How to Get There: Take the M6 and leave at Junction 40. Go along the A66 to Cockermouth Sheep & Wool Centre. Take a left on to the A5086 to Egremont. At the end of the A5086 turn left at the roundabout onto the A595 and follow the Barrow signs. Go through Calderbridge and New Mill until you come to sign for Gosforth, Eskdale and Wasdale, then turn left into Gosforth.

Additional Information:
- Bookings can be made online at the hotel's website
- The hotel offers seven double en-suites, one single en-suite and 'The Copley Suite'. Each of the rooms is unique, with exposed beams, and a number of rooms retain their original fireplaces
- The bar offers a friendly and relaxed atmosphere, supported by a good range of wines, spirits and locally brewed real ales
- The menu includes a selection of homemade pies that the hotel has become famous for
- The restaurant itself is set within the original hall and booking is recommended
- Gosforth Hall Hotel caters for birthdays, christenings, weddings and conferences

Hardknott Roman Fort

Hardknott Fort was known to the Romans by the name Mediobogdum and was one of the loneliest outposts of the Roman Empire. It was built between AD 120 and AD 138, during the reign of Emperor Hadrian, and is positioned on a spectacular site overlooking one of the steepest roads in the UK. The drive up the steep, narrow, winding road is not for the faint of heart but, along with the incredible scenery, this makes for the incredible experience that is Hardknott Roman Fort.

Initially the fort was occupied only briefly, before being abandoned during the Antoinine advance into Scotland in the middle of the second century. The fort was reoccupied in the late second century and was in use until the end of the forth century, during which time the garrison was a detachment of 500 men from the Dalmatian coast (infantry soldiers from Croatia, Bosnia-Herzegovina and Montenegro).

The Romans built a road over the pass in the second century and called the road the Tenth Highway. It reaches a height of 1,289ft at the summit of Hardknott Pass. The road fell into disrepair when the Romans left England in the early part of the fifth century, although it remained a popular route for packhorses in the centuries that followed.

The ancient Roman road was completely destroyed during the Second World War, when the Ministry of Defence used the area for tank training. A decision was made to rebuild the road using tarmac, but the current road was not built on the exact route of the Roman road it replaced.

The fort is one of the best preserved Roman remains in Cumbria. The fort is 375ft square and covers an area of around 3 acres. The stone-fronted rampart has been partially rebuilt from stone reused from the site, with a slate course distinguishing

Hardknott Roman Fort. (By kind permission of English Heritage)

the original stonework from the rebuilt stones. The rampart wall is in the region of 12ft thick. In each corner of the fort are the foundations of corner towers and on all four sides are the remnants of gateways. Within the walls of the fort the granaries, soldier's barracks, Commander's House, and headquarters building (or *Principia*), have all been excavated and the surviving stonework preserved.

Outside of the walls of the fort is the bathhouse. This consists of three adjoining rooms; the cold room (*Frigidarium*), the warm room (*Tepidarium*) and the hot room (*Lacoricum*).

Higher up the hill is a large parade ground, evidence of the strict military discipline that the garrison lived under. The ground has been levelled and on its west side is a ramp leading to a viewing platform, for the officer commanding the military exercises. The parade ground is considered the finest surviving example in the Western Empire.

The remote location of the fort, with dark crags above and below, gives Hardknott Fort a very eerie atmosphere. There is an old legend that says the site is home to a fairy rath where King Eveling held his court. This legend dates back to at least 1607, when William Camden wrote of the link between Hardknott and the fairies in his book *Britannia*.

In more recent years Hardknott Roman Fort has been home to some unusual paranormal activity, including whispering in visitors' ears, dark shadows, and strange sounds. In 2003, on a glorious summer's day, over a dozen witnesses saw a strange swirling mist slowly rise from ruined fort, before moving swiftly in the directions of the Commander's House; it then dispersed as suddenly as it appeared.

On the 8 May 2007 a couple were at the ruined fort alone when they heard the sound of marching boots on a hard surface, even though the area was covered in grass. The footsteps lasted around thirty seconds before fading away.

Visitor Information

Telephone number: (0870) 3331181
Email: customers@english-heritage.org.uk
Website: www.english-heritage.org.uk/daysout/properties/hardknott-roman-fort

Opening Hours: Hardknott Fort is accessible at any reasonable time.

How to Get There: The fort is 9 miles north-east of Ravenglass, at the west end of Hardknott Pass.

Additional Information:
- Hardknott Roman Fort may not be accessible in winter months as icy and snowy conditions make the pass too hazardous
- Dogs are allowed on leads
- There is parking at the fort
- There are no facilities at the fort

Kirkstone Pass Inn

*T*he Kirkstone Pass Inn stands in a lonely, windswept position, 1,489ft above sea level. It is the highest occupied building in Cumbria and the third highest inn that England has. The building dates back to 1496, when it was a built as a private house, and was restored in 1847 having fallen derelict. At this time it opened as an inn called the Traveller's Rest. It was renamed the Kirkstone Pass Inn at the beginning of the twentieth century. The site on which the building stands was previously that of a monastery.

The Kirkstone Pass Inn is named as such because of the Kirkstone Pass, the summit on which it is situated. It is very popular with tourists and walkers alike, and provides breathtaking views over the Lakeland Fells and Brother's Water (a lake at the bottom of the pass). The A592 runs through this pass (the highest pass open to traffic in the Lake District) and links Ambleside to Patterdale in the Ullswater Valley. The pass rises steeply, climbing 1,300ft in just 3.5 miles, with a gradient of 1 in 4 in places. It is known locally as 'The Struggle', a name dating back to when horse-drawn coaches would struggle with the incline and require passengers to climb out of the coach and walk to the top on foot.

The poet William Wordsworth, who lived in the nearby village of Rydal, walked this pass many times. He described the pass most evocatively when, in 1817, he wrote 'The Pass of Kirkstone', which includes the lines:

> When, through this Height's inverted arch,
> Rome's earliest legion passed!
> They saw, adventurously impelled,
> And older eyes than theirs beheld,
> This block-and yon, whose church-like frame
> Gives to this savage Pass its name.
> Aspiring Road! that lov'st to hide
> Thy daring in a vapoury bourn,
> Not seldom may the hour return
> When thou shalt be my guide.

The name of the pass is derived from a nearby stone named the Kirk Stone; it is found on the left bank above the road as it descends from the summit close to the inn. The old Norse word for a church is 'kirk', and the stone is roughly 4ft high and resembles early steep-roofed Norse churches.

There are records going back hundreds of years of people dying while attempting to traverse the Kirkstone Pass in adverse weather conditions. The weather in the Lake District is not to be underestimated, as it can change from one extreme to the other in a matter of moments. The weather on the Kirkstone Pass can be particularly bad

The Kirkstone Pass Inn. (By kind permission of The Kirkstone Pass Inn)

during the winter and sometimes, in extremely snowy or icy conditions, the pass is closed off by the police as it is simply too dangerous. It may well be that this tragic loss of life has contributed to the Kirkstone Pass Inn's reputation as the most haunted public house in the North West; so paranormally active, in fact, that in 2007 the BBC *Countryfile* magazine listed it as the fourth most haunted country pub in Britain.

The most regularly reported spirit is that of Ruth Ray, one of the many victims of the treacherous mountain pass. She was a young mother living in the area in the early eighteenth century. She was at home caring for her newborn son, when she received news that her father was gravely ill at his home in Patterdale. It had been snowing that day but the skies were blue, so, in a state of worry for her father, she wrapped her baby up warm and set off across the pass. Ruth was not wealthy and she had no way of traversing the pass other than by foot. To Ruth's horror mist descended onto Kirkstone Pass and this was followed by a blizzard.

Ruth's husband feared for her safety so headed out into the blizzard to try and bring her home safely. He tried to follow the same route but the weather was deteriorating further and he realised that his own life was in danger. He would have perished on the pass had it not been for a sheepdog that led him back to the safety of a nearby farmhouse. The husband was eager to head back out into the night but realised that he would surely die. He hoped and prayed to God that his beloved wife and child had made it safely to her father's before the blizzard had set in.

The following morning he headed back out onto the pass, this time accompanied by the farmer and the sheepdog. They found Ruth and his son close to the top of the pass; she was dead, holding her son tightly in her arms. The man collapsed onto the snowy ground, distraught with the grief of losing the two most important people in his life, his wife and his son, who was only a few weeks old. However, the farmer shouted to him that his son was still alive. It was a miracle, but sure enough the tiny child was perfectly fine. In Ruth's final act before the blizzard claimed her life, she had removed her shawl and wrapped it around her baby before holding him close to her chest; she knew she stood no chance of surviving but hoped that she may be able to save her son.

Tragically, she died only a short distance from the summit, at which point she would have been able to find warmth and shelter in the building which is now the Kirkstone Pass Inn. The despair that Ruth must have felt knowing that she was going to die must have been incredible, and she has haunted the area around the inn ever since, especially in snowy conditions. Through the window of the inn people have seen the figure of a woman outside, cradling a baby in her arms; others have seen the dark figure of a woman appearing to be searching for something. Late at night people leaving the inn, or spending the night there, have heard a baby's cry carried on the wind across the pass.

In the summer of 1993, a visitor took a photo of his family in the porch of the inn and, when he developed the film, he realised he'd captured something impossible. Behind his smiling family stood a man who had not been present at the time the photo was taken. He was a tall male figure wearing the attire of a seventeenth-century coachman. The spirit has been seen several times since inside the inn, and is known as Nevill.

In the nineteenth century the Kirkstone Pass Inn was one of the first coaching inns along the busy trade route to and from Scotland, and a young boy of ten years old, Nettle, was the son of the inn's carriage master. Nettle loved to meet the travellers as they came through the pass, and used to wait close to the summit for the sound of approaching wagons and horses coming up the steep, snaking, road. However, one day his enthusiasm cost him his life. He ran out into the road to greet the wagon, but it didn't slow down and knocked him to the ground; the accident killed him. The wagon didn't stop at all and headed on past the inn.

Nettle's ghost remains at the Kirkstone Pass Inn and has been blamed for the pranks that regularly befall the staff and guests. Lights turn themselves off and on, and doors that should be open are found to be locked. On other occasions all of the chairs have been stacked on top of tables during the night, and pictures have been taken down from the walls and stacked neatly on the floor.

Visions of coaches being pulled up the pass by teams of horses, and the sounds of horses trotting past in the middle of the night, have been reported, but when the witness looks out of the window to see the source of the noise, there is nothing there.

A malevolent entity lurks within the inn; a phantom, which exudes evil though its intentions are unknown. Belief in this 'thing' is taken so seriously that talking about it within the pub is forbidden. One night, after the pub had closed, two members of staff were counting the takings when they clearly heard footsteps on the floorboards above them, but they were the only people in the building. Taking a dog with them, the two men headed upstairs unaware of what they would encounter. When they reached the top of the stairs the dog sat down, began to whimper and would go no further. The two men were extremely nervous and each encouraged the other to go first. Their hearts pounded as they opened the door of the first room and peered in, scanning the room with their torches, but they found nothing. They opened the second door and again it was empty. They were extremely nervous now, as whatever lay in wait for them had to be in the third and final room; there was no other way out of the building. They burst in simultaneously, just in time to see a black figure move swiftly across the room and vanish into a wall. Neither man knew what it was but both experienced the same feeling – that it was pure evil and the most terrifying thing either of them had ever experienced.

One local taxi driver won't even enter the pub, despite regular calls to pick people up from the inn. He had an experience so disturbing a number of years ago, whilst inside, that he won't even talk about it. He has vowed to never, ever go inside the Kirkstone Pass Inn so long as should he live.

Behind the inn is a tree that was used in the eighteenth century to execute criminals. Dozens of men and women met their death at the end of a rope dangling from that tree, and because they were not allowed to be buried in consecrated ground, their bodies were thrown onto the fells to decay and be feasted upon by insects and animals.

One local, who died in this manner, was a former owner of the building. He was persecuted by the local villagers, following the mysterious death of his twin baby sons. There was no evidence to support their belief that the father had any involvement in their sudden deaths, and he appeared to be genuinely devastated, but the villagers decided that there was no doubt that he had murdered them and decided to take the law into their own hands. They dragged him to the hanging tree and tightened a crudely constructed noose around his neck. As he dangled from the tree he was crying huge tears of grief; not for his own impending death but for the loss of his sons, who he had not even had the chance to bury. Ever since his death his spirit has been seen outside the Kirkstone Pass Inn, mourning the death of his children for all eternity.

Visitor Information

Address:
The Kirkstone Pass Inn
Ambleside
Cumbria
LA22 9LQ

Telephone number: (015394) 33888
Email: inn@kirkstonepassinn.com
Website: www.kirkstonepassinn.com

Opening Hours: Monday to Saturday 11 a.m. – 10 p.m., Sunday, 11 a.m. – 6 p.m.

Food served daily from midday – 3 p.m. and 6 p.m. – 8 p.m., and on Sunday from midday – 5 p.m.

How to Get There: Follow the A592 from Ambleside up 'the Struggle' and you will find the Kirkstone Pass Inn close to the summit.

Additional Information:
- Four en-suite rooms are available with full English breakfast for guests looking to stay overnight
- All rooms have tea and coffee making facilities and a DVD player as there is no television reception. There is a selection of DVDs to watch, including *The Kirkstone Ghost Story*
- For those on a budget, you can book a bed in the bunkhouse (sleeps twelve). The bunkhouse has a shower and central heating to ensure you're warm no matter the weather outside
- Home-cooked meals are made with locally sourced ingredients. All meals are cooked freshly to order, and groups of six or more are advised to book ahead. There is also an impressive vegetarian menu
- The bar serves a number of the pub's very own award winning local ales
- When the weather is cold outside, the inn's traditional open fire will keep you cosy inside. In warmer months there is outdoor seating offering a fabulous view
- There is a car park opposite the Kirkstone Pass Inn

Levens Hall

*L*evens Hall began life as a simple pele tower in 1350, built by the de Redman family to defend against the threat of attack from the Scots. It had cattle byres below ground level and under-housing for the women and children to take shelter in times of trouble. The tower remained in the de Redman family until the 1550s when their successors, the Bellinghams, chose it as their main residence. In 1578, James Bellingham began building a comfortable family home around the tower; this work was completed in 1641, over fifty years after he started. This was also the year in which James Bellingham died.

In 1694 Colonel James Grahme added a fine staircase leading from the Great Hall, the brewhouse, and the east and south wings. Grahme had won the house in 1688 from his cousin, Alan Bellingham, a compulsive gambler, on the turn of a card; the ace of hearts. Shortly after taking ownership of Levens Hall, Grahme had waterspouts added to the front of the hall; they were marked with hearts and the initials of himself and his wife.

Colonel Grahme was a close friend of King James II, and Grahme filled the house with grand furniture including the superb Charles II dining chairs, which remain to this day, and many beautiful works of art. In the late 1690s, he employed French garden designer Guillaume Beaumont to create the topiary gardens, which

Levens Hall at Christmas. (Photograph provided courtesy of Levens Hall)

are Levens Hall's most famous feature, attracting thousands of visitors each year. The gardens remain almost unchanged over 300 years later.

With over 600 years of continued occupation, it may come as no surprise that the Bagot family, who live at Levens Hall today, share their home with all manner of things that go bump in the night.

A Grey Lady is regularly seen walking the ancient topiary gardens after dark and is believed to be the ghost of a pregnant gypsy woman, who cast a curse upon Levens Hall at the beginning of the eighteenth century. It was a wild winter night, and the gypsy woman was weak, freezing and starving; she approached Levens Hall begging for shelter, but was turned away. She was so weak that she collapsed and died where she lay in front of the hall. But before she took her last breath she cursed the family, warning that no eldest son of the family would inherit Levens Hall until a white doe was born in the hall's deer park, and that the waters of the River Kent would freeze over.

For almost 200 years the estate passed down the female line; that was until 1895 when the curse was finally broken. In this year a pale-coloured fawn was born to one of the black Norwegian deer that lived in the acres of park land in the grounds of Levens Hall; there was also a particularly severe winter which saw the nearby River Kent freeze. The following year, a son was born to the Bagot family and named Alan Desmond and, in 1913, he inherited Levens Hall from his father.

Despite the curse being broken, the sinister wraith of the Grey Lady is still the most commonly reported ghost. She is described as having her lank hair tied up in a bun, wearing a long purple-grey dress with the ragged hem hitched clear of her bare feet. As well as in the gardens, she has also been seen at the bottom of the drive, close to the river. In 1973 she was almost the cause of a near fatal accident, when she suddenly appeared in the middle of the road in front of a motorist; he had to slam his brakes on to avoid her. In recent years she crossed the road in front of a cyclist, who fell off his bicycle trying to go around her; when he looked up to check he had not caught the grey-looking lady, she had vanished.

Another well-reported phantom is that of a small playful black dog. The origin of this friendly ghost is a mystery, but he is described as being small and woolly with bright friendly eyes. He enjoys playing on the staircase, confusing visitors by running around their feet as they climb the stairs, causing people to trip up and try to avoid standing on him as he appears so solid and real. He then vanishes suddenly. At other times people will open a door and the little dog will rush out to greet them wagging his tail, but when someone attempts to stroke the dog their hand passes straight through him.

Another unidentified spirit at Levens Hall is that of the Pink Lady; a benign ghost who was first seen in 1973, when two separate groups of visitors clearly saw the figure of a woman standing on the staircase wearing a long pink dress, an apron and a mob cap, similar in style to an eighteenth century maid. Ever since, the Pink

Lady (as she has become known) has been seen regularly on the staircase and also walks along the hall, appearing to be solid. Witnesses have commented on how she seems to just suddenly 'dissolve'.

In the 1950s, a priest called Father Stonor was making a visit to Levens Hall to visit an ill member of the Bagot family. He let himself in and as he passed the main hall he saw a man playing the harpsichord, with a bright electric light burning above them. Not wanting to disturb the man he continued past him and headed upstairs to comfort the family member. After twenty minutes they had dozed off into a peaceful sleep, so he quietly made his way back downstairs where the harpsichordist was still playing. Again he did not disturb the man and was about to leave when he heard voices coming from a nearby room. He knocked and entered to find the lady of the house, Mrs Bagot, with guests, having a candlelit tea party. He made conversation and asked, in passing, why they were sitting in candlelight; he was told that there had been a power cut and the electricity was out. The priest was a little confused about this and explained that he had passed a man playing the harpsichord, who was sitting under a perfectly functional electric light. The lady of the house assured the priest this was not possible and, trying the electric light switch again to show the power had not been restored, she explained that the only member of the family who could play the harpsichord was her husband, who was away on business. The priest led her out into the hallway to find silence and darkness; the man had vanished.

Mrs Bagot was now gravely concerned for the safety of her husband, as she believed every word the priest had said and was now worried that it may have been her husband's ghost, or some kind of warning that he was in danger. However, having no mobile phones in those days, she had no way of contacting him. Father Stonor had not met Mr Bagot before, so could not confirm whether it was the husband that he had seen playing the instrument or not.

Thankfully, Mr Bagot returned home safely the next day, as did Father Stonor. But to the priest's horror, he immediately recognised Mr Bagot as the man he had so clearly seen the previous day. He even asked Mr Bagot to play the harpsichord, only to hear that the piece of music he played was the exact same one he had heard him play the day before.

The present owners of Levens Hall experience strange noises and ghostly apparitions. Mr Bagot's mother-in-law had her very own encounter whilst staying overnight at the hall; awaking in the middle of the night, she was witness to three apparitions standing at the foot of her bed. The figures were that of a man with a stick and a woman with a small child. The guest, whom Mr Bagot described as a rather forthright woman, simply asked the trio of spectral visitors, 'What on earth are you doing here, get out of my bedroom!' With this the three figures turned and walked into a wall

The figure of a young girl has been seen hiding amongst the trees in the topiary gardens on several occasions since she was first reported in 1992, during a paranormal investigation. In the same investigation, flashing lights were reported to have illuminated the gardens inexplicably, a phenomenon that continues to this day.

During the writing of this book, I was fortunate enough to be able to track down a former paranormal investigator from the highly popular Living TV series *Most Haunted*. The show investigated the hall back in 2002 and ghost hunter David Scanlan told me about his experiences investigating the ghosts of Levens Hall:

> I remember my time at Levens very well indeed. It was my first time investigating with the *Most Haunted* team, but I have been investigating the paranormal independently since I was eleven years old and, since 2001, with the Hampshire Ghost Club, a group I formed to investigate claims to the paranormal.
>
> I was aware of the well-known stories associated with Levens Hall, but something that really intrigued me was a recent sighting by the owner's son. He had awoken in the night and opened his bedroom door to visit the toilet and was rather taken aback when he witnessed a black shrouded figure silently gliding down the corridor towards him. The young lad promptly closed his door and jumped back into bed and ignored the need for his bathroom break.
>
> I remember the night being a mixture of random electromagnetic fluctuations, temperature differences and a general overall awareness of what might be. The most interesting occurrence during the investigation came at a time for me when the team had downed tools for the night and decided to get some sleep. I carried on my investigations and ventured around various parts of the hall on my own. At one time I was sat in silence and became aware of a female presence. I know the readers will immediately start by saying 'not another bloody psychic', but I would like to point out that I am quite a scientifically-minded person and not in the least bit psychic, as far as I am aware. Regardless, this presence came very close and all of a sudden I just felt an overwhelming sensation of causing sadness to the family; not on a nasty level but on the level of an illness that toppled a once strong personality. The feelings I had, physically, I could only liken to those of a stroke. I decided to leave the area in the hope that it would clear the presence with me, but it didn't. I ventured out of the hall and the feeling just intensified. The feeling finally went when I returned to the hall and I came to rest in a small area no bigger than a box room, just off of a room where the family kept a copious amount of silverware. That's when the feeling finally left me and I felt I had dropped the woman off to an area in which she felt comfortable. I still can't explain the sensations or the occurrence. Derek Acorah, our spiritualist medium on the show, told me it was a form of possession and a way in which to convey what the spirit was feeling and trying to say to people.
>
> It has been nearly a decade since I had this experience and this is the first time I have revealed it. I don't know why now – it just feels that now is the time for this experience to be firmly recorded so the event can be researched further and maybe help someone else who has experienced something similar.

Visitor Information

Address:
Levens Hall
Kendal
Cumbria
LA8 0PD

Telephone number: (015395) 60321
Email: houseopening@levenshall.co.uk
Website : www.levenshall.co.uk

Opening Hours: The opening times change annually; please visit the hall's website for up-to-date opening dates and times.

The gardens, gift shop and Bellingham Buttery open at 10 a.m. and the house opens at 12 noon. Last entry to the house is at 4 p.m. The house closes at 4.30 p.m. and the gardens close at 5 p.m. Levens Hall and Gardens are closed Fridays and Saturdays unless there is a special event.

How to Get There: Leave the M6 motorway at Junction 36 for the A590 (signposted 'Barrow-in-Furness) then take the A6 south (signposted 'Milnthorpe'). Levens Hall is signposted from here.

Additional Information:
- The Bellingham Buttery offers a wide range of delicious home-cooked food, with a daily blackboard menu of hot and cold dishes, puddings and snacks. A vegetarian option is always available
- There is a living-willow labyrinth within the topiary gardens. In the centre of the maze a hare can be found
- There is a children's play area
- There is a gift shop
- A collection of steam vehicles can be seen
- Discounts may be given for groups of over twenty people, although it is advisable to book in advance

Muncaster Castle

*T*he lands at Muncaster were granted to Alan de Pentitone in 1208 and, over 800 years later, they remain in the Pennington family. The castle was built in 1258 by Gamel de Muncastre. The foundations of the castle stand upon Roman remains dating back to around AD 79; the site was chosen by the Romans due to the strategic importance of guarding the River Esk. The name Muncaster contains the Latin word *castra*, meaning 'fort' or 'military encampment'.

The oldest remaining part of the castle is the pele tower, a type of fortified watch station that was common in the English-Scottish border region, built in around 1325. Peace between the two countries had ceased in 1296 and the county town of Cumberland, as it was at the time, was the target of many Scottish raids. Few Scottish prisoners were taken at Muncaster Castle, but those who were suffered in dark, dank cells. There was little money spent on providing for them; many starved to death and others attempted, in vain, to prologue their own life by eating the dead.

In 1463, Sir John Pennington sheltered the fugitive King Henry VI after defeat at the Battle of Hexham. Having been refused hospitality at nearby Irton Hall, the

Muncaster Castle. (By kind permission of Muncaster Castle)

King was found sheltering from the elements by some shepherds, who took him to Muncaster where he was welcomed and given shelter. The King was so grateful that he presented John with a small bowl made of green glass and decorated in gold and white enamel; this bowl has become known as the Luck of Muncaster. The King claimed that as long as this cup remained unbroken, the Pennington family would prosper and never lack a male heir. Henry went on to explain that this cup was his own holy-water stoup. Unfortunately for the King his own luck was to run out shortly afterwards. He had lived a very stressful life, littered with periods of insanity; being the only child of Henry V he had succeeded him to the throne as King of England in 1422, at the age of nine months old. He was returned to the throne in October 1470, a reign which lasted less than six months, as in the April of 1471 he was imprisoned in the Tower of London, where he died during the night of the 21/22 May. It was said that he had died of grief having heard that his son, Edward of Westminster, Prince of Wales, had been killed on the 4 May at the Battle of Tewkesbury. It is widely suspected, however, that his successor, Edward VI, who was crowned the morning following Henry's death, ordered his murder.

The castle was extended, rebuilt, and redesigned with almost every generation of Pennington, but by 1770 the castle, under the ownership of Sir Joseph Pennington, was no longer occupied. His son, Sir John Pennington was wed in 1778 and decided to make the castle a home for his new family, but when he arrived to inspect the castle he was dismayed with how ruinous the once-grand house had become; so much so that parts of the building collapsed as he was inspecting it. He invested £6,000, a huge sum of money at the time, to rebuild and restore the castle; this included changing the Great Hall into a dining room.

In 1783, Sir John had a three-storey octagonal tower built as a monument to King Henry VI, a mile north-east of the castle. It is said to mark the spot where the shepherds found the King wandering alone 300 years earlier.

In the 1830s, the castle's north tower was built to complement the pele tower and to provide a symmetry to the appearance of the castle. In 1862 Gamel Augustus Pennington, the fourth Baron Muncaster, employed fasionable architect Anthony Salvin to oversee alterations and further rebuilding of the castle. Salvin covered the courtyard and converted it into the present drawing room, as well as altering the twelfth-century Muncaster Church within the estate.

Today the Muncaster Castle stands within an estate covering 1,800 acres, 77 of which are fabulous woodland gardens containing plants from all over the globe, including flowering shrubs from the Sino-Himalayan region. Each passing season sees the gardens awash with colourful foliage, and in 2009 the *Independent* newspaper voted Muncaster Castle number one in its list of the top fifty 'Best Spring Days Out'.

John Ruskin described it as 'the gateway to paradise'. This is a view that the majority of visitors to Muncaster Castle are likely to share, but for others this couldn't be further from the truth; some visitors encounter something so dark, so terrifying, that they flee from Muncaster in abject fear, vowing never to return. It is this occurrence, which happens all too often, which has earned Muncaster Castle the reputation of being one of the most haunted castles in England.

Scientists have been investigating Muncaster since 1992, and have found Muncaster Castle so fascinating, and some of the occurrences so inexplicable, that they are still working alongside the owners to try and explain the cause of the paranormal phenomena, which are reported on almost a daily basis.

Muncaster's best known ghost is that of Tom Fool, a close friend of William Shakespeare, whose real name was Thomas Skelton. He was a steward and jester at Muncaster Castle during the late sixteenth century and the word 'tomfoolery' derives from his name. A magnificent portrait of Tom, holding his Last Will and Testament, can be seen within the castle.

Despite the usual idea of a jester as someone fun and innocent, Tom is one of the darkest, most despicable, characters in the history of Muncaster Castle. He is said to

The portrait of Tom Fool. (By kind permission of Muncaster Castle)

Tom Fool's tree. (By kind permission of Muncaster Castle)

have been responsible for countless deaths with one of his cruel jokes; he would sit beneath a large chestnut tree and guide anyone who asked for directions towards some nearby quicksand, rather than sending them the correct way. Some of them realised in time to save themselves from probable death but many were never seen again.

Tom's master was Sir Ferdinand Pennington. He paid Tom to kill a local carpenter who his daughter, Helwise, had fallen in love with. Tom relished the task, disposing of the poor carpenter brutally and, to prove the unwelcome suitor had been taken care of, he hacked his head from his shoulders to take back to Muncaster Castle and present to his master. Ever since this evil murder was committed, the ghost of a man without a head has haunted the tapestry room of the castle.

Ironically, it is said that Tom died in around 1600, in the very quicksand to which he had sent so many to their death. He was drunk and took a wrong turn when he was on his way to the castle late one night; his body was never recovered. Tom Fool's spirit remains about the castle, lingering and watching. Most of the ghostly happenings are attributed to him; however, with the myriad of other phantoms that reside within Muncaster's ancient walls, any of them could be to blame.

The ghost of King Henry VI is said to have haunted Muncaster Castle since his death in 1471, as this is one of the few places where he experienced security and felt welcome. He is said to be active in the room in which he was hidden, and the carved-oak bedstead in which he slept remains in the same room to this day.

The tragic ghost of Mary Bragg can often be seen wandering the grounds of the castle and along local roads. Mary was a pretty young housekeeper in nearby Ravenglass at the turn of the nineteenth century. She fell in love with an Irish man in his thirties, who worked as a footman at Muncaster Castle. Mary was madly in love with this man and he occupied her every waking moment; she was the happiest woman in the world. Unfortunately for Mary he was not the man she thought, as he had a string of other lovers in the locality.

Mary's attention became so great that one of her rivals for the man's affection decided to take action. In the winter of 1805, two local men were persuaded to dispose of Mary for the cost of a night's drinking. Late one night, the two men went to the modest cottage that Mary shared with her parents and knocked on the door. Mary answered wearing only her night clothes and slippers and the men told her that her lover had been injured badly in an accident and was crying her name, desperate to see her. Her heart began to pound in her chest as she feared for the man she loved, so, despite the late hour, she grabbed her shawl and followed the men out into the night. They took her towards Muncaster Castle on a horse and cart while she wept bitterly, eager to find out the severity of her beloved's injuries. As they neared the castle they took a sudden detour into dense woodland and stopped.

Mary was confused; she stepped down from the cart demanding to know why they had stopped when Muncaster Castle was so close; she was so desperate to be at her lover's side. Her anger turned to fear as the two men began to approach her. One of them demanded she shut up and punched her, knocking her to the ground. They dragged Mary, who was now in a hysterical state, to a large tree and both men began to sexually assault her as she screamed out for help. The men knew that there was no chance of anyone being near enough to hear her at this hour.

After the men had carried out their evil attack on Mary, she fell to the ground crying her heart out in shame and disgust; the men simply laughed at her. She prayed that this would be the end of her ordeal, but the men had not finished yet. One of them grabbed her by the head and smashed her face into the tree while his accomplice laughed and cheered him on. Mary screamed and begged for her life, but the attack continued; her face was rammed into the tree time and time again; her nose was smashed apart and she could no longer see. Unsure of whether she had been blinded or if she could not see due to the amount of blood that was gushing out of her face, she felt faint and was close to passing out. Finally one of the men picked up a large rock and brought it down on the top of her head; her suffering was brought to an end as she was killed immediately.

A few weeks after Mary's mother had reported the disappearance, her body was found in a badly decomposed state floating in the River Esk. Identifying the body proved difficult as eels had eaten away at Mary, leaving an empty hollow where her face once was. Her murderers were never caught.

Witnesses have reported seeing her appear as a melancholy White Lady, who spends eternity searching for the man she loved so dearly, a man who never truly deserved her love.

Other haunting reports relate to a man who was thrown from the pele tower in a row over hunting rights in the 1380s. He had ascended the tower to point out the land owned by his family and was thrown to his death. There have been several sightings of a man seen falling from the tower over the last century, but when witnesses rush to the area where the man should have hit the ground – expecting to find a grisly scene of death – there is no sign of a body.

The tapestry room has gained notoriety in recent years and is believed to be the paranormal epicentre of the castle. Babies have been heard crying, children have been heard singing nursery rhymes, and the soft comforting voice of a lady has mystified visitors as well. It is said that one of the children could be the spirit of Margaret Susan Pennington, who died of screaming fits at a young age in 1871. There is also a claim that many years ago, three children, who were sleeping in the room that is now the tapestry room, vanished during the night and are now buried within the walls. For many years the link between the sounds of children and the tapestry room proved to be a mystery, however James Cartland, archivist and family friend, uncovered some plans from the nineteenth century, which show that during the extensive rebuilding work that started in 1862, part of the old nursery was incorporated into the present-day tapestry room.

The door handle of the tapestry room had been reported to rattle and turn as if someone is trying to get into the room, but when investigated there is never anyone there. The temperature in the room is also extremely unstable; it has been known to plummet within mere moments, getting so cold that even on a summer's day visitors have been able to see their breath. Also cameras and mobile phones have turned themselves on and off inexplicably.

The Frost-Pennington family, who live in the castle today, will not spend the night in the tapestry room. Peter Frost-Pennington has even been quoted as saying, 'I've lived here twenty years and in all those years I've never dared sleep in the tapestry room; I'm not that stupid.' Even during the day, visitors with no prior knowledge of the tapestry room's reputation have suffered panic attacks and have complained of chest pains. At night, the room comes alive and seems to attempt to envelop anyone brave enough to face its atmosphere, with the pure evil that seems to reside there. Several visitors, who have attempted to get to sleep in the room, have quickly found it to be the worst night's sleep they are ever likely to get, if they manage to get to sleep at all. Some have been alarmed by a large black figure standing over them as they lie in the antique four-poster bed; often they

The Tapestry Room. (By kind permission of Muncaster Castle)

also experience a heavy weight on their chest stopping them moving or crying out. Others have been dramatically thrown from their bed.

In 2008, a group of experienced paranormal investigators visited Muncaster, but none of them would stay in the room alone. Twenty minutes into their investigation the group all saw the black shadow of a child walk through the room. The investigation ended after just twenty-one minutes.

It is possible to spend the night in the tapestry room on a ghost sit, and many brave visitors have chosen to do so with some spectacular results. Here are some notes from the reports taken on these overnight vigils.

Approximately 1 a.m. a high-pitched growl/whine heard near the window, heard again around 1.40 a.m., one of our group felt someone grab the back of his neck. At 2.40 a.m. the noise heard again. Near 4 a.m. a baby was heard crying. Very peculiar and strange but definitely there!

January 2003

A definite presence could be felt in the room. The temperature would suddenly drop as if an ice cold presence had entered the room. Some of the group felt cold down one side. Could hear scraping noises coming from fire, and a noise like someone playing a flute.

June 2004

I spoke to Sue Dent, who is the Hospitality Director at Muncaster Castle. She told me that she isn't sure if she believes in ghosts, but recounted two experiences to me:

After a wedding one Saturday evening we were clearing up. The wedding party had used the croquet set on the front lawn during the day, and I decided to take it back to the North Tower for storage. The passageway and entrance way was very gloomy but not black-dark and, because I wasn't bothered in the slightest and could just about see, I didn't put a light on. The key to the large downstairs-storage room is difficult to turn as the lock is upside down.

I propped the croquet set against the wall and took hold of the round door knob, which was loose, and I tried to turn the key, which wouldn't budge. All of a sudden the door knob turned in my hand which gave me a real start and possibly started my hackles rising a bit. Anyway, I persevered and took hold of the door knob again, only to find it rock solid. My mind went into overdrive then; I left the croquet set where it was and legged it extremely quickly!

On another occasion we had outside caterers looking after the wedding guests in the dining room and I was on my own in the Great Hall. It was evening and dark outside and I was sitting in a large chair at the bottom of the room on my own. The shutters were drawn in the Hall and I was reading a book. I glanced up to my right and saw a flash of light streak from the guard room entrance and go across the room to the entrance to the library. I can only describe it as a sort of sideways lighting, gone in a flash! I kept looking up quickly to see if it would happen again but it didn't and I wasn't upset by it.

Archaeologist Clifford Jones appears to have awakened a new spirit, to add to the already impressive list of hauntings at Muncaster. He has been investigating the Roman boundaries around Muncaster Castle. One night he was staying in the pele tower, the oldest part of the building, and heard the sound someone chopping wood, but only he and the lady of the house were in the castle.

Clifford went outside into the darkness of the night and tried to head towards the source of the noise, which appeared to be coming from the site of one of the trenches he was excavating. He couldn't see anyone so shouted, 'please stop making that noise,' and it stopped immediately.

He was a little spooked by this so ran back inside. He entered the first room he came to, the bathroom, which had a light on. As he stepped inside, the light bulb blew and so he went back onto the landing and continued to climb the tower. He came to a well-lit landing, but the light bulb blew here as well. He then went to the lounge and when he flicked the light switch all the bulbs in the room blew. He was

The library. (By kind permission of Muncaster Castle)

so scared by what had happened that he fled the castle, only finding the courage to return three days later.

The BBC heard of the happenings around the archaeological dig and contacted Para.Science to help investigate the unusual occurrences further. I spoke to Ann Winsper, one of the founders of the group, and she told me of what lay in store for them at Muncaster Castle:

Our investigation into Muncaster Castle was prompted by a call from the BBC – usually when we investigate a location we arrange a long-term plan, as this allows us to firstly observe the location at different times of day, different times of year, different weather conditions etc. It also allows us to 'get a feel' for the building – each building has its own peculiarities, creaks, groans, draughts etc. We also normally try to replicate the conditions described by witnesses when an apparent paranormal event is reported – there is no point sitting in the dark at 4 a.m. if the ghost is reported as appearing at 3 p.m. in the afternoon while the witness was doing the washing up! Muncaster has quite a history of apparent paranormal activity and, with it being a spectacular old building, it is impossible to remove the expectancy factor when bringing a group of people in.

We were originally called out as the archaeologists working on site had reported some strange happenings. Whilst working in the courtyard, they reported a sense of something being around them all the time, although they never caught a glimpse of anyone or anything. There had also been reports of sounds and odd noises coming from the cellar area.

Sadly due to circumstances beyond our control, we were not able to stay in these areas to carry out an overnight investigation; however, we visited the basement and spent some time in the courtyard area. Nothing unusual occurred, however both areas did seem to have an atmosphere that could easily unnerve an unsuspecting visitor, especially once dark fell.

As these areas would also prove difficult to investigate with the television cameras, it was decided that the BBC reporter would be asked to spend the night in the reportedly haunted tapestry room. We checked the room over and nothing appeared unusual, but the room is quite atmospheric, with it being old, having uneven floors and portraits hanging on the wall – all the ingredients of a classic haunted room.

The reporter retired to bed in the early hours, and we monitored the room with equipment, including cameras. After ten minutes lying on the bed, we were surprised to see the reporter leap out of bed and run off down the corridor as if the devil was after him! Once we had calmed him down and spoken to him, he described feeling very uncomfortable in the room, a feeling which progressed to sheer terror, causing him to flee at speed. He was obviously very shaken up, but we could find no evidence on either camera of anything unusual happening. Our team bravely volunteered to spend the rest of the night in the tapestry room, but nothing unusual happened; in fact I managed a few hours sleep whilst lying on the bed.

It is impossible to ignore the atmosphere in a place such as this. None of our group reported feeling scared or uncomfortable, but the weight of history certainly affects how people respond to buildings; a brief shadow glimpsed out of the corner of the eye is given a very different significance when glimpsed in an old haunted castle than when glimpsed in a modern flat.

After dark there has been the sound of growling coming from the castle grounds, also the shadow of a huge cat-like creature has been seen; this is attributed to a lion shot by the last Lord Muncaster whilst in Kenya, with the skull returned to the castle as a trophy.

Visitor Information

Address:
Muncaster Castle
Ravenglass
Cumbria
CA18 1RQ

Telephone number: (01229) 717614
Email: info@muncaster.co.uk
Website: www.muncaster.co.uk

Opening Hours: The exact opening dates vary annually, so please consult the website for up to date opening times.

The Castle is open for 'Christmas at the Castle' on Saturdays and Sundays from late November until late December, 1 p.m. – 3 p.m.

How to Get There: The castle is located 1 mile south of Ravenglass, along the A595. Follow signs for the Western Lake District from Junction 36 of the M6 motorway.

Additional Information:

- For those brave souls prepared to face Muncaster's infamous tapestry room, the castle offers ghost sits for groups of up to 6. However, due to the extreme nature of the spirits residing within the room all participants must be over seventeen years of age. Your visit will begin late evening with a private tour of the castle, in which you will hear of all the ghosts and legends of Muncaster, just to set the scene for the night which lies ahead. The following morning you will greeted by a full English breakfast in Creeping Kate's Kitchen
- There are regular overnight ghost vigils led by the scientific research team who have been investigating the hauntings at the castle since 1992. Full and current information can be found on the website or by calling the castle
- There are special ghost walks in the week leading up to Halloween; these are extremely popular and booking in advance is essential. Tickets can be booked on the website
- The Festival of Fools is an annual event lasting five days. Madness and mayhem is guaranteed as performers flock to Muncaster from all across the globe, performing acts of comedy, magic, and acrobatics
- Experience the magic of Muncaster decorated for Christmas, with music and special effects transforming the gardens to a winter wonderland
- Creeping Kate's Kitchen is open daily from 10.30 a.m. – 5.30 p.m. and serves a full selection of food. Last orders for meals is approx 4.30 p.m., with cakes, coffee and tea available until 5.30 p.m.
- Souvenirs to remind you of your visit to Muncaster Castle can be bought from the Owl Shop or the Carriage House Gift Shop and Information Centre
- In the MeadowVole Maze the grass is seven feet tall. Voices are provided by Harry Enfield and the maze is dark in places, so adult supervision is recommended
- Muncaster's World Owl Centre, home to the World Owl Trust, has the largest collection of owls on Earth (over forty species), from the tiny Pygmy Owl to the huge European Eagle Owl. Daily flying displays are held on the castle lawns

Nenthead Mines Heritage Centre

The Nenthead Mines Heritage Centre is the largest lead mining complex with public access in the UK. It is in the village of Nenthead on Alston Moor, and was the first purpose built village in the country. Nenthead is also the highest village in England.

During the eighth century the mine was a major producer of silver and lead, and Nenthead was the first village in England to develop electric street lighting. This was only possible due to the power generated within the mines.

In the seventeenth century, individuals and small companies owned mining leases in the area and sold their ore for smelting to the Ryton Company, who were based near Newcastle-upon-Tyne. The Quaker-controlled Ryton Company merged with the Governor & Co. in 1704, forming the London Lead Company, often called the Quaker Company due to many of the shareholders being Quakers. In 1715 the Manor at Alston Moor was seized by the Crown as the owner, James Radcliffe, the 3rd Earl of Derwentwater, was executed for his part in the First Jacobite Rising. In 1735 the land was granted to the Royal Hospital for Seamen at Greenwich. The mining leases at Alston Moor were let to Colonel George Liddell in 1736 and the first smelting mill was built. By 1745, the London Lead Company had taken over the leases from Liddell and began to mine Nenthead.

The London Lead Company operated the mine at Nenthead until 1882, when the Nenthead and Tynedale Lead and Zinc Company took over. Silver production was increased and smelting continued for fourteen years, until the Belgian firm, the Vielle Montagne Zinc Company, took over the site in 1896. The site was modernised and ore continued to be mined until the last of it came out, in around 1920. Production slowed, the spoil heaps were reworked and, eventually, work ceased at the mine in 1965 and the site was abandoned. The buildings were left to decay and collapse for over thirty years until 1996, when the North Pennines Heritage Trust bought the land and began the restoration of the buildings. The Heritage Centre was opened to the public on the 15 July 1996, by John Craven. The Carr's Level Mine was restored and opened for mine tours in July 2000.

The life of a miner was a difficult one, and what with spending eight hours a day underground in cramped and wet conditions, it was also a dangerous one. The average age of a miner was forty-five; many would lose their lives to a disease they called 'the black spit' (Anthracosis), which was a lung disease caused by inhaling dust from the mine. Once a miner began coughing up the black liquid, he knew that there was nothing a doctor could do to help; death was sure to follow.

The miners of the day used to believe the mines were haunted by spirits called Knockers. It was believed that they were the spirits of souls trapped between Heaven and Hell, and cursed to live below ground for eternity. The miners believed that the Knockers lived in the deepest, darkest parts of the mine and they were blamed for any distant creaking or knocking. Miners' belief in Knockers was a tradition across the country, but we will never know if they truly believed that the mine was haunted or were merely adhering to tradition. However, what we do know is that the Nenthead Mines Heritage Centre is undoubtedly one of the most paranormally active locations in Cumbria today.

The phenomena reported at the centre, since it opened in 1996, has been frequent, varied and terrifying; disembodied footsteps have been heard by visitors in many of the buildings throughout the centre, and in the Assay House in particular. Light anomalies, often known as orbs, are also regularly seen floating in some of the buildings, even in broad daylight.

Animals have refused to enter some of the buildings, their eyes appearing to follow something moving which is unseen to human eye, often followed by barking and growling. This has also been reported at the entrance to Carr's Level Mine.

Within the mine, voices have been heard when no one else has been present, stones have also been thrown at visitors by unseen hands. Perhaps most inexplicably of all are the impossible reports that the emergency telephone system, which is based within the depths of the mine, has called to the surface – of course, no one is in the mine at the time.

The entrance to Carr's Level Mine. (By kind permission of the North Pennines Heritage Trust)

A recreated waterwheel built for the visitor centre.
(By kind permission of the North Pennines Heritage Trust)

Steve Taylor, of Alone in the Dark Entertainment, led an investigation at Nenthead Mines Heritage Centre on the 24 April 2010 and told me of the amazing occurrences that he experienced that night:

We arrived at around 7 p.m. and had a walk around the site. There was snow still on the hills and it was bitterly cold.

The investigation began at around 10 p.m. and straightaway things began to happen. The First odd thing was that during the introduction we heard a loud commotion outside the room we were in; there were lots of men shouting and it sounded like people fighting and a panic, even what sounded like horses. We could see out all around us and the door was open to the room. We rushed out and nothing, not a person in sight! The moors were just dark and cold with only the souls of the dead.

Shortly afterwards I was carrying out a walk around with a medium and I saw a pair of legs on a modern, man-made bridge. Just a pair of legs in dark trousers and boots, but there was nothing visible above the waist. They walked around a corner and then dispersed into thin air.

Disembodied footsteps have been heard throughout many of the outbuildings.
(By kind permission of the North Pennines Heritage Trust)

During a séance in one of the downstairs office rooms the Ouija board went crazy and the air temperature dropped from 9 °C to -2 °C, and remained at -2 until the Ouija board stopped. At the precise moment the Ouija board stopped it was accompanied by the office door opening and what sounded like footsteps leaving the room. During the séance we also heard what sounded like a man's voice speaking in a language none of us could understand. We have since found out that Italian miners lived in this room. After the séance Alison Dunn, our medium, picked up on a blocked tunnel under the same room and explained that a man was trapped and died within the tunnel and his skeletal remains are still there. We had no knowledge of this and it was later proved to be correct.

Within Carr's Level Mine it is damp, cold, and very dark.
(By kind permission of the North Pennines Heritage Trust)

While in Carr's Level Mine, we were hit by stones thrown at us, heard footsteps that could not be explained, and saw some strange bright lights when all lights were off.

Steve Taylor's team continued their investigation into the night and encountered yet more chilling paranormal experiences:

We used the Assay House as our hub for the evening and we recorded some great EVPs (Electronic Voice Phenomena). We asked 'when where you here?' and had a reply which sounded like five or six different voices trying to speak over one another, but the answer we recorded sounded like, 'yes, 16, 33, 27.' We also asked 'did you die here?' and recorded a man's voice saying 'yes killed.' We left the room shortly afterwards, but left a locked-off video camera in the room.

We were joined by local radio station Spark FM close to midnight, and they witnessed a bright flash from the Assay House as they were stood outside. It was described as being like a bright explosion with no sound.

At this point I took a break and got chatting to a mine explorer who was staying at the Mill Cottage Bunkhouse with his friend. He told me that he had been to the pub earlier for a meal and a drink, and when he got back to the bunkhouse he was about to walk up the staircase when he saw the dark figure of a man reach the top of the stairs and go around the corner. He spoke to the man thinking it was his roommate, as he took his boots off. The figure did not reply and he heard a door shut. He walked up the steps and to the bedroom; when he opened the door the lights were out. He was in total darkness, so he turned the lights on and asked his friend if he was alright with the light being on. He looked towards his friend's bed and there was no one else in the room with him, despite him clearly seeing someone walk up the stairs ahead of him, and then heard this door close. He was shook up so left the building to get some fresh air, and this happened just before he started talking to me. After he'd told me this story he asked why my group and I were here and why we were up so late. I explained that we were investigating the ghosts of Nenthead Mines. The blood from the guys face drained away and he turned white!

During an Ouija board session in the hub things took a turn for the worse, and things really began to happen. At first the Ouija board was weak, and kept stopping, but then the table started to rock and tip becoming more aggressive and powerful, and this was a 6ft-long table! A spirit identified itself as being called Emily and she said that she died in the mine in 1936. She also told us that she was nineteen years old when she died. At this point we were interrupted by our radio, and we were told that a guest investigator, Tony, had entered the Carr's Level Mine with the guys from Spark FM.

At this point the planchette went crazy; it went really fast in a circle then spelled out the words 'bad', then 'evil', then, to our abject horror, it spelled out 'die Tony, die Spark FM.' It then explained there was something evil in the mine and they would 'die tonight'. At one point we all took our fingers off and it still kept moving; it was becoming so powerful. At this point we decided to close the séance down.

This brought an end to our night, and we were later told of many, many sightings of dark figures in the mine, and disembodied voices heard constantly.

Visitor Information

Address:
Nenthead Mines Heritage Centre
Nenthead
Alston
Cumbria
CA9 3PD

Telephone number: (01434) 382726
Email: mines@npht.com
Website: www.npht.com/nentheadmines

Opening Hours: The opening hours change annually, so please visit the centre's website for opening times.

The centre is also open every day of the week, all year round, to pre-booked groups of ten or more.

How to Get There: The centre is signposted from the A689 road, close to Alston.

Additional Information:
- There is a charge to visit the mine, which includes the mine tour. There is a reduced charge for visitors who are over sixty, and pre-booked groups of ten or more
- Minimum height restrictions apply for the mine visits. The mine is unsuitable for wheelchair access
- Wear suitable shoes if you plan to take the mine tour. The mine can be damp and cold in areas, even in the summer months
- There is free car parking
- A gift shop and café can be found in the centre
- There is an area to pan for minerals for a small charge
- There is a picnic area within the historic courtyard of the Heritage Centre
- There is an extensive range of self-guided trails throughout the 200 acre site, including heritage trails and nature trails
- The Assay House and Mill Cottage Bunkhouses are the perfect base for your visit to the North Pennine area. The rates are £12.50 per person per night and the bunkhouses are open all year
- Alone in the Dark Entertainment organise a range of ghost walks, public paranormal investigations, and even a ghost hunting course. For more information please visit www.aloneinthedarkentertainment.com

Souther Fell

Souther Fell, the most easterly of the Northern Fells, stands at 1,713ft and offers staggering views across the Pennines. It is famed the world over for having one of the best, if not the best, authenticated ghost story of all time. The stories of Souther Fell's ghosts date back to 1735, when a farmhand, Daniel Stricket, standing half a mile from the fell on Midsummer Eve, was astonished to see a spectral army on the eastern side of the peak. They appeared to be very well disciplined and marched five abreast, with officers on horseback riding back and forth along the ranks. He watched for over an hour as they marched east to west, until they disappeared in turn through a dark cleft on the summit.

He told his story to William Lancaster, the owner of Blake Hills Farm on which he worked. Not surprisingly he was disparaged from repeating this story to others as they both knew that the sides of Souther Fell are perpendicular slopes, making it impossible for an army to march upon it. However, word of Stricket's 'ghost army' got out to the local villagers and he was ridiculed. Despite this, Stricket never changed his story and insisted that he had seen an army of thousands upon the fell.

Exactly two years later, on Midsummer Eve 1737, the phantom army were seen again, this time by William Lancaster, the farmer who had rejected his farmhand's claims so vehemently on the previous occasion. William rushed into the farmhouse and shouted for his family to come and see. They stepped outside into the twilight to see what all the excitement was about, only to be dumbfounded when they too saw legions of soldiers marching silently over the inaccessible mountain top. They

Souther Fell.

watched in awe for over an hour until darkness descended and blotted out the amazing scene. William told Stricket that he had also seen the army, and when word reached the local villagers he was lambasted in the same way his farmhand had been two years earlier.

In 1743, a Wilton Hill farmer and one of his employees reported witnessing a man and a dog on Souther Fell chasing some horses. Suddenly the man, dog and the horses all disappeared over a precipice without a sound. The men ran over to see if they could help, but the search turned up nothing at all; it was as if they'd just simply vanished.

On Midsummer Eve 1745, ten years after Daniel Stricket first saw the phantom army, William Lancaster was desperate to witness the sight once more, and this time he was determined to ensure that the villagers saw it too. He went to Wilton Hill and rounded up twenty-six people to accompany him to his farm to await evening and, hopefully, the return of the spectral army. Sure enough, around the hour of 8 p.m., the army returned, this time interspersed with carriages. One witness timed the occurrence and it lasted for over two hours. So convinced were many of them by what they'd seen, that they scaled the fell the following day looking for footprints, horseshoes and carriage tracks; however, they found no evidence that the army had even been there. Every single witness knew what they had seen and they agreed that they were prepared to swear it before a magistrate. Forty years later, in 1785, two survivors put their names to an attestation of what they had witnessed on that evening.

Not since the sighting of 1745 has the phantom army of Souther Fell been seen again.

Visitor Information

How to Get There: Access to the fell can be found nearby Low Beckside, to the east.

Additional Information:
- Appropriate footwear is essential for any visitor
- The walk up and down the fell is likely to take around three hours, with the summit being around a mile in length. The highest point is indicated by a pile of rocks known as a cairn

Talkin Tarn

*T*alkin Tarn Country Park, located close to the historic town of Brampton, is named for the 60-acre glacial tarn that lies within. The word 'tarn' is derived from the old Norse word *tjörn*, meaning 'small lake' or 'tear drop'. Talkin Tarn was formed 18,000 years ago, when the colossal force of moving glaciers scoured huge scars and holes into the landscape, and then filled them with the water of the vast melting glaciers. Today the tarn is fed by natural freshwater springs.

It would be easy to envisage that the 165-acre woodland of the country park could be home to all manner of paranormal oddities, especially after dark when the visitors have long since dispersed and absolute darkness descends. The woodland takes on a far more sinister appearance at this time. The country park does appear to be active, as there have been reports of unusual flashing lights coming from the dense woodland in the early hours of the morning. The sound of galloping horses approaching from behind has also been heard by visitors on the gravel path that surrounds the lake; however, when the startled visitor turns around there is nothing there and the sound stops as suddenly as it began.

Despite this reported phenomenon, it seems that the lake itself is the hub of the activity at Talkin Tarn Country Park. The cause of these happenings may be related to the grisly legend of Jessie, who lost her life beneath the murky depths of the tarn. In the 1850s, Jessie was in love with a wealthy man, who she believed loved her just as much. She wanted to tell his mother of their love but he prohibited this, as he was also engaged to a rich land owner's daughter, who Jessie knew nothing about. Jessie decided that she wanted to share their special love with the world and, in particular, with her family, but

Talkin Tarn.

the man begged her to keep it secret. She refused and told him she was going to tell regardless of his wishes; he even offered her money to stay quiet, but she would not agree to it. He relented and told her that if she wanted to tell her family and friends he would be delighted to go with her. He told her to meet him at Talkin Tarn that evening so they could tell her family together, and Jessie, overjoyed, threw her arms around her true love.

They met at the lakeside that evening and they kissed eagerly. Before long they were passionately intertwined next to the lake, the water lapping at their bodies. As they were lost in the throes of passion, he held her head under the water while still on top of her and Jessie panicked; she fought with all of her strength to get free of his grasp, but she was a petite young lady and she never stood a chance. He held her head under the water for several minutes, and she became increasingly less able to fight, until she stopped moving altogether. He then took her lifeless body and placed it in three sacks. He dug a shallow grave a few feet from the shore and put her into it, replacing all the mud and rocks on top. Jessie's body was never recovered.

To many this may seem like nothing more than a legend; however, in the September of 2002, twenty-three people witnessed the bloody apparition of a young lady walking from the lake in broad daylight. This made front page news in the area and many believe it could have been the restless, heartbroken spirit of poor Jessie.

The area around Talkin Tarn also appears to be home to UFO activity. I was there in 2002 and a taxi driver told me that one night, a couple of years earlier, he had been driving from Brampton train station into Talkin when he saw a bright green flying object land in a field; apparently it looked like a beach ball. On his return journey out of Talkin, he saw a figure standing at the side of the road which he could only describe as looking like a spaceman, and in its hand was a gadget that appeared to resemble a metallic umbrella. Suffice to say he didn't hang around for long.

The Blacksmiths Arms in the very early hours of the morning, on the day of Halloween 2002. Could the glowing white figure in the downstairs window be the spirit of Maggie, the former landlady? (Photograph by John Crozier)

Visitors in search of the paranormal at Talkin Tarn would be advised to stop off at the Blacksmiths Arms public house in the village of Talkin. It is said to be haunted by the spirit of a former landlady called Maggie Stobbart. Reports of glasses moving around the bar are common, and there have also been regulars who swear they have seen a full apparition of Maggie.

Visitor Information

Address:
Talkin Tarn Country Park
Tarn Road
Talkin
Brampton
Cumbria
CA8 IHN

Telephone number: (016977) 41050
Website: www.carlisle.gov.uk/talkintarn

Opening Hours: Talkin Tarn Country Park is accessible at all times.

The tearoom is open seven days a week 10 a.m. – 4 p.m.

How to Get There: Talkin Tarn is 1.5 miles south of the town of Brampton. It is signposted from the A69 at Brampton.

Additional Information:
- There is a boathouse, tearoom and gift shop
- Toilets and baby changing facilities are available
- There is an education cabin / meeting room for schools and groups
- Boat hire is possible at weekends and during school holidays, from Easter to October half term, weather permitting
- Fishing is allowed on Talkin Tarn (day tickets can be purchased). The close season is 15 March – 5 June inclusive. Rowing boats can also be hired for fishing by prior arrangement
- There is a choice of short woodland trails varying in length
- A bird-feeding area can be found on the site
- Camping is allowed in the small camping field. Groups must pre-book and have liability insurance
- The tearoom, toilets and log cabin are all wheelchair accessible

Triermain Castle

Triermain Castle, sometimes called Gilsland Castle, was built in 1340 on top of a small glacial mound, after King Edward III had granted Sir Roland de Vaux a licence to crenellate. It was built with stone reclaimed from Hadrian's Wall. It is quadrangular in plan, with towers on the west and east sides, and would have been enclosed by a curtain wall and a moat. Its purpose was to defend the Barony of Gilsland (or Guilsland as it would have been known at the time) from attacks by the Border Reivers and, in particular, the Armstrongs and Elliotts.

During the reign of King Edward IV, the castle passed by marriage into the hands of Sir Richard Salkeld and, by 1510, it was in the ownership of Lord Thomas Dacre. The castle was abandoned in 1569 and a report from 1580 described the castle as being in 'ruinous condition'. The tower was demolished in 1688 and a considerable section of the remaining castle collapsed in 1832, with the stone being used to repair adjacent farm buildings.

All that remains of Triermain Castle.

The main internal building measured 22m by 21m, but only a single corner survives; this is the south-east corner of the gatehouse. It would have originally stood at a little over 9m high, and is still nearly its original height.

The castle was perhaps the inspiration for Sir Walter Scott's poem 'The Bridal of Triermain', written in 1813. It tells of King Arthur's daughter, Gyneth, being sentenced to eternal slumber by Merlin. Five hundred years pass and Sir Roland de Vaux, the creator of Triermain Castle, learns of the legend of Gyneth and sets out on an epic quest to find her and win her hand.

The ruinous castle is said to be the home of a tragic spirit known as the Shivering Boy. The tale dates back to the fifteenth century and is about a six-year-old boy who inherited the castle when his parents passed away. His uncle became his guardian, but he was a cruel man and wanted Triermain Castle for himself. He led the young boy out onto Thirlwall Common in the middle of a winter storm, and the boy died in the snow. However, the child returned to the castle in death, haunting the family who lived in the castle which was rightfully his. He would walk the halls in the dead of night, touching the family members with his icy fingers as they slept, his teeth audibly chattering all the while. Then, most terrifying of all, they would feel him sit upon their bed and say in a whispered voice, 'cauld, cauld forever more', before vanishing. The castle, as it was in the fifteenth century, is all but destroyed, but it is believed that the Shivering Boy still haunts the remains to this very day, and if you are out amongst the ruins late at night you may feel his icy touch.

Visitor Information

How to Get There: The castle is on the B6318 road, 5 miles north-east of Brampton.

Additional Information:
- There are no facilities at Triermain Castle

Wastwater

*I*n the Wasdale Valley, in Cumbria, is Wastwater, a dark, deep and very mysterious lake. It is an example of a glacially 'over-deepened' valley. It is 3 miles long, half a mile wide and around 260ft deep. Wastwater was voted 'Britain's Favourite View' by viewers of ITV in 2007, and is a favourite with photographers. It is unusual for a day to go by without the sight of keen photographers, arriving in their dozens, waiting patiently to capture the perfect shot a couple of hours before dusk. The lake is surrounded by the mountains of Red Pike, Kirk Fell, Great Gable and Scafell Pike. The water is cold and is home to trout and the ancient arctic char, which have survived since the Ice Age.

Reports of a monster residing in the murky depths at Wastwater first appeared in the early 1960s, when water pipes were placed into the lake for a nuclear-plant cooling system, at what is now Sellafield nuclear power station. Word began to spread; workers from the project told of seeing a long dark 'something' swimming in the depths of the lake, moving like a fish but much, much larger, claiming it to be several metres in length.

The lake has become popular with divers, and stories of a monster living at Wastwater have remained prevalent. In December 2002, one witness told *Diver* magazine of his encounter with the creature:

> Anybody who has ever dived England's deepest lake, the eerie Wastwater in west Cumbria, knows that there's something very large and very strange down there. I saw it move off into the depths, way below me, when I was at 36m in wonderfully clear water in the early '80s. Sceptics would say I was full of narcosis. I say I saw something the size and shape of a giraffe head off into the deep. When you stop laughing,

Wastwater is a breathtaking sight and was voted Britain's favourite view in 2007.

consider this fact: there are little fish in Wastwater left behind by the retreat of the last Ice Age. Perhaps something higher up the food chain was left behind with them.

In the early 1980s, a spiritually sensitive visitor to Wastwater described the lake as being filled with the dead, and explained that they could feel the hollow eyes of the dead staring up towards the surface. In 1984 a body was discovered in the lake by a diver, Neil Pritt; it was the remains of Margaret Hogg. Margaret's husband, Peter, was arrested and confessed to her murder. Margaret had been having an affair and Peter strangled and killed her in October 1976. He wrapped her lifeless body in a carpet and tied it to a block of concrete, before dumping it in the lake. The body lay undiscovered for almost eight years and, due to the lack of oxygen in the water, it had not decomposed; it had been preserved like a wax-work model.

It is believed that there may be many more undiscovered bodies at the bottom of Wastwater; the police are restricted to diving to a maximum depth of 50m, and the lake is 79m deep. Margaret's body was discovered at a depth of 38m, on a ledge only a few centimetres away from a drop that would have seen her body reach the bottom of the lake, never to be discovered.

Visitors in search of the supernatural in Wastwater may want to visit nearby Wasdale Corpse Road. As Wasdale had no church early in its history, the dead had to be transported over the fells to Eskdale for internment, leading to this route becoming known as the Corpse Road. This road is said to be haunted by a spectral horse carrying the body of woman. Her son had died and whilst his body was being carried along the Corpse Road on a misty day, the horse carrying his body bolted and was lost. His mother was heartbroken, knowing her son's tiny body would never be laid to rest; she herself died shortly after. Tragically, her son's body was found shortly after she passed away and was given a full Christian burial. As the mother's body was taken over the fells to Eskdale, a terrible snow storm descended suddenly and the horse was lost in the blizzard; her body was never found. It is said that this woman haunts the Wasdale Corpse Road to this day, and that she is unable to rest due to the torment she feels, believing her son was never given a proper burial.

Visitor Information

How to Get There: Wastwater is on the A595 past Nether Wasdale. Care needs to be taken on the narrow country roads.

Additional Information:
- There is an area for parking at the side of the road next to Wastwater
- There are no facilities at Wastwater, but there are plenty of villages nearby offering refreshments

Windermere

Windermere is England's largest natural fresh-water lake, covering an area of 5.69 miles and reaching a maximum depth of 67m. The lake is a ribbon lake, which means that it is long and narrow; Windermere is over 11 miles long and just under a mile in width at its widest point. The lake also has eighteen islands, the largest of which is the privately owned 40-acre Belle Island.

Windermere was formed over 13,000 years ago during the last Ice Age. It was created when a glacier dug a glacial trough through a vein of soft rock, then, as the glaciers melted, the trough filled with water to make Windermere.

Windermere is undoubtedly one of the country's most popular locations for family breaks and holiday homes, as every year thousands flock to the area to enjoy the natural beauty that Windermere has to offer. This has been the case since the Kendal and Windermere Railway first built a line to the area in 1847. The name Windermere is believed to originate from 'Vinandr's Lake' (from the old Norse name Vinandr and 'mere' meaning lake). It was known by the name Winandermere until the mid-nineteenth century.

Far from the fun and laughter of the glorious summer days enjoyed by holidaymakers at the lakeside, are the continued reports of strange, howling cries coming from Windermere and the surrounding area after dark. These happenings date back over 100 years, the earliest recorded occurrence coming in 1895. This year saw a particularly harsh winter and the entire lake froze over. Locals said that every night, for over a week, they heard loud, continuous moaning noises and cries coming from beneath the frozen surface. Some people passed it off as the sound of cracking ice being carried on the wind. Some believed it to be the tragic ghosts of forty-seven wedding guests, who were aboard a ferry on the lake on the 19 October 1635. The over-laden vessel had sank beneath them and every single passenger drowned. A more common belief amongst locals is that it could be the phantom Crier of Claife, the spirit of a monk from Furness Abbey who is said to make himself heard by crying out over the waters of Windermere.

The legend of the Crier of Claife tells of how a monk fell in love with one of the women who came to Furness Abbey in search of help. However, the love he felt for her was not returned and she rejected him. Heartbroken, he made his way to Windermere and to Claife Heights, a wooded area on the western shores of the lake. He cried out into the night's sky a wild outpouring of grief, and then he fell to the ground, dead, having lost the will to live.

On a stormy night, several months later, a local ferryman heard the cries across the lake and mistakenly thought it to be someone calling out for his services. When he returned without a passenger he was visibly shaken; he was as white as a sheet, his eyes were wide in their sockets and he was unable to speak. He took to his bed and died within days, having never been able to tell of what he had seen that night. Following this it was not possible to get a ferry across Windermere after dusk, as the other ferrymen were terrified of coming face-to-face with the Crier. The cries continued night after night, and a priest was called to exorcise the terrible phantom. Although the terrifying wails of the Crier ceased, the area of Claife Heights continues to have an uneasy atmosphere. On more than one occasion, packs of foxhounds, in full cry during a hunt, have stopped dead in their tracks when they come near to Claife Heights; whimpering, they were unwilling to continue the hunt.

There are also a number of spectral animals linked with Windermere; there have been many sightings, since the 1500s, of a phantom white horse, which witnesses have seen gliding across the surface of the lake from shore to shore. Legend has it that anyone who witnesses the white horse will suffer a death in their family shortly afterwards.

Another mythical beast linked with Windermere is the Tizzie Wizzie. The first sighting of the creature is attributed to a boatman at Bowness, who used to regale tourists in the early 1900s with stories of his encounters with this strange,

Windermere at dusk. (Photograph provided by Natalie Johansen – unconsciously-me.blogspot.com)

water-loving creature. It had the body of a hedgehog, the tail of a squirrel and a pair of wings similar to that of a bee. Although this sounds like a fanciful tale, fabricated to entertain children, sightings of Tizzie Wizzies have been regular; reports of encounters have been given as recently as 2008.

On 23 July 2006, Windermere hit the headlines in newspapers nationwide, when University lecturer Steve Burnip and his wife, Eileen, were horrified to see what they could only describe as 'a Loch Ness-type monster' at the north end of the lake, swimming close to the shore. At the time Mr Burnip told the *Yorkshire Post*:

I was on holiday at Dower House at Wray Castle. It was the first Sunday of a week-long holiday, around lunchtime. I was walking along the lake with my wife and two friends and we'd walked up to Watbarrow Point, which juts out into the lake about 40ft above the water. We were just stood chatting and I literally saw it – similar to the classic three lumps that you get in the Loch Ness pictures; I could see a head with swirling water and then a grey lump, more swirling water, and another grey lump. But the most remarkable thing was that it was really moving. My jaw just dropped open and I said 'Look at that!' My wife also saw it, but very quickly it moved up the lake. I estimated it to be at least 30ft long. I wouldn't believe anyone else if they told me – but I saw it and know what I saw.

In March 2007 the lake monster of Windermere was spotted again, this time by photographer Linden Adams, who christened the beast 'Bownessie'. He was walking in the area with his wife when they spotted it. 'It just came out of the blue,' said Mr Adams:

The water was incredibly peaceful and then this huge thing appeared, diving and thrashing around. It appeared to be 50ft long when I compared it to the nearby boats. I snatched the binoculars from my wife and gasped when I got a better look. I could see this huge dark thing moving in the water. It had a head like a labrador, only much, much bigger.

In July 2009, Thomas Noblett was swimming in the lake when he was suddenly swamped by a 3ft wave. Mr Noblett was training daily on the lake for a channel swim and had never entertained the idea that the lake monster may actually exist, but he was at a loss to explain the sudden bow wave. He was swimming at 7 a.m. and his swimming trainer, Andrew Tighe, was in a boat alongside him; they were the only people on the lake. He commented:

We had gotten up early and Windermere was crystal clear. The lake was totally empty apart from us, and all I could hear was the slapping of my arm against the water. All of a sudden this wave just hit us. Andrew asked where the hell the wave had come from and it made the boat rock from side to side. It was like a big bow wave; a 3ft swell at least. There were two, as if a speed boat had sped past, but there were no boats on the lake.

I spoke to Jon Downes, the Director of the Centre for Fortean Zoology (CFZ), about Bownessie, and he told me of several other eye witnesses, who contacted the CFZ with reports of the Windermere monster following Mr Burnip's report, which brought the creature to the media's attention:

An incident was reported by a Mr and Mrs Gaskell, who had seen the creature whilst boating on the lake in July 2006. The weather was dry and fine, with little breeze, and the surface water was warm and calm. They have, on many occasions, seen fish jumping and surfacing in the lake, but on this particular day they were travelling at around 4 knots near the yellow 6m/h marker at the entrance to the Ambleside basin, at the north end of the lake, when they both saw a disturbance in the large surfacing water, about 20 yards astern. Mr Gaskell told me that they had seen something very large surfacing and diving again, which looked like a seal or dolphin without the fin, leaving a large wake and ripples. They did not see it again that day, or anything similar since.

Over the next month we received six further eyewitness accounts. Interesting, one was from the late 1950s, and another from the early 1980s. The other contemporary sightings followed in much the same pattern as Mr Burnip's, but – for me at least – the most exciting account came from Kevin Boyd, an amateur diver, who is extremely conversant with the wildlife in the area, and has seen eels of 6ft in length on a number of occasions, both in Windermere, and in the neighbouring lake of Coniston Water.

Visitor Information

Address:
National Park Visitor Centre
Windermere
Cumbria
LA23 1LJ

Telephone number: (015394) 46601
Email: hq@lake-district.gov.uk

How to Get There: Brockhole (The National Park Visitor Centre) is situated on the east shore of Lake Windermere, midway between Windermere and Ambleside.

Additional Information:
- Situated between Windermere and Ambleside, Brockhole has a magnificent lakeside setting offering fun for all the family, including: an adventure playground; exhibitions; fabulous gardens; an information centre; gift shop and café
- More information on CFZ can be found at www.cfz.org.uk

About the Author

Rob Kirkup was born in Ashington, Northumberland in 1979. He developed a keen interest in the paranormal from an early age, amassing a large collection of books and newspaper cuttings on the subject and, in particular, stories of supernatural happenings in the north-east of England.

In 2002, Rob led a paranormal investigation at Talkin Tarn (a haunted lake in Cumbria) as part of Alan Robson's 'Night Owls' Halloween show' on Metro Radio. In the years that have followed Rob has conducted investigations at some of the North's most haunted locations, including Hylton Castle, Woodhorn Church, the National Railway Museum, Flodden Field, Chillingham Castle, and the Castle Keep. Rob's first book, *Ghostly Northumberland*, was published in 2008, and was followed by *Ghostly Tyne and Wear* in 2009, and *Ghostly County Durham* in 2010.